CONTEMPORARY'S

ATTRACTIONS

TEACHER'S GUIDE

ETHEL TIERSKY
MAXINE CHERNOFF

CB

CONTEMPORARY
BOOKS

CHICAGO

Published by Contemporary Books, Inc.
Two Prudential Plaza, Chicago, Illinois 60601-6790
Manufactured in the United States of America
International Standard Book Number: 0-8092-3684-2

10   9   8   7   6   5   4   3   2   1

Published simultaneously in Canada by
Fitzhenry & Whiteside
195 Allstate Parkway
Markham, Ontario L3R 4T8
Canada

CONTENTS

TO THE INSTRUCTOR

"Places that tell stories" is the unifying theme of Contemporary's four-book reading series, *Attractions*. These twenty-four stories describe fascinating places that many Americans hope to visit some day. As students read to increase their awareness of U.S. history and geography, they strengthen a wide range of linguistic skills—reading, writing, listening, discussing, researching, debating, and even dramatizing.

A controlled reading level and highly visual format combine to make this series particularly suitable for developing adult readers. *Attractions* is especially appropriate for intermediate English as a Second Language students as a tool to help them develop cultural literacy and improve their language skills.

CONTENTS OF THE READERS

The six readings in each volume are connected by a common theme.

- Book One, *It's Colossal*, is about some of the country's greatest giants: the Statue of Liberty, Sears Tower, the Gateway Arch, Mount Rushmore, the Grand Canyon, and Walt Disney World.

- Book Two, *Back to the Past*, focuses on places that make American history come alive. They include Plimoth Plantation, the White House, New Orleans, the San Francisco Bay Area, the Vietnam Veterans Memorial, and the commonwealth of Puerto Rico.

- Book Three, *Sun and Games*, highlights states, cities, and sites that attract large numbers of tourists. Included are Las Vegas; Elvis Presley's home, Graceland, in Memphis; New Mexico; Hawaii; Hollywood; and Minnesota.

- Book Four, *Birthplaces of Ideas*, concerns places where notable Americans accomplished great things. Sites included are philosopher Henry David Thoreau's Walden Pond; the North Carolina coast where the Wright Brothers flew the first airplane; Thomas Alva Edison's New Jersey laboratories; Martin Luther King Jr.'s birthplace and final resting place, in Atlanta; architect Frank Lloyd Wright's Wisconsin home, Taliesin; and environmentalist Rachel Carson's native Greater Washington, D.C.

INSTRUCTIONAL DESIGN

Each nonfiction reading is short—about 2,000 words. The reading level for each book has been certified at 5.0–5.5 on the Dale-Chall modified scale. The text is divided by subheads, each of which is followed by comprehension questions that allow students to check their understanding periodically. These questions may be used for class discussion, small group discussion, or as writing activities. Other notable elements of the series include the following:

- a full-page photograph that introduces each selection
- a pre-reading teaser that piques students' interest, motivating them to read the selection
- phonetic spellings of foreign and unfamiliar words and names
- difficult vocabulary defined in context or glossed at the bottom of the page
- photographs and diagrams that provide the visual stimulation developing readers need
- a Sidelights page that provides brief, interesting facts about the topic or locale of the reading
- post-reading activities on making inferences, practicing vocabulary, and group discussion
- an answer key for the post-reading activities at the end of each book

ABOUT THE TEACHER'S GUIDE

Our comprehensive teacher's guide provides teaching tips and strategies, suggests extension activities, and lists supplemental teaching materials for all four books in the *Attractions* series. This guide has been designed so that teachers with limited experience in teaching reading skills can comfortably use the series. Strategies for presenting each of the twenty-four stories are provided as are ideas for expanding upon the readings. However, teachers are provided maximum flexibility in choosing strategies that are appropriate for the needs of their classes. Following the two pages of strategies are six pages of reading and language exercises for each selection. Of these six pages, exercises on phrasal verbs and other idioms, pattern practice, and phonics and pronunciation are especially useful for ESL students. These exercises can be reproduced for homework or for in-class practice.

PRESENTATION STRATEGIES

In the teacher's guide, instructional material that corresponds to each story is grouped under the categories **Pre-Reading Activities**; **Activities to Accompany the Reading**; **Discussion, Writing, or Research Topics**; **Extension Activities**; and **For ESL Students**.

The **Pre-Reading Activities** include questioning strategies that allow students to share knowledge and experiences that they bring to the topic. The teacher, too, can share stories about travels and can bring to class visual aids that will help the students relate better to the places, people, and times covered in the reading. Encouraging students to look at the opening photos, asking them to make predictions based on title and section headings, and challenging them to guess the answers to the teasers all are strategies to stimulate interest, introduce vocabulary, and, in general, make the subject matter come alive.

The material in the category **Activities to Accompany the Reading** offers ways to have fun with the information from the reading. Suggestions for word games and role-playing are offered, in addition to opportunities for comparing and contrasting, improvising scenes, and debating.

Discussion, Writing, or Research Topics provides focused opportunities for students to express their reactions to the material presented.

Extension Activities are suggestions for using the reading as a springboard for additional assignments. For example, topics for library research and writing are listed. Related material such as videotapes, recordings, and films are recommended.

For ESL Students highlights language and cultural literacy issues that are of particular importance for ESL students.

REPRODUCIBLE EXERCISE PAGES

The exercises in Contemporary's *Attractions* series cover all aspects of reading—from word recognition and meaning to relationships between ideas. Important reading skills, such as getting word meaning from context and understanding inferences are practiced extensively. Reproducible exercise pages are provided for the following skills:

- reading comprehension and reading skills
- vocabulary practice
- words in context
- homonyms, synonyms, and similar words
- parts of speech and inflected forms
- word parts
- phrasal verbs and other idioms
- pattern practice
- phonics and pronunciation

The last three items in this list are especially useful in the ESL classroom. More space is devoted to reading comprehension and reading skills in Books Three and Four than in the earlier books. Furthermore, in these two books, the students are required to write sentences more often than in the others.

Finally, the exercises provided in this teacher's guide are designed to encourage success. In many exercises, the students are provided with the number of the paragraph or paragraphs that contain the answers to the questions. The wide range of skills developed in the *Attractions* series should give students a greater ability to comprehend new reading material. And all of this is accomplished as students enjoy high-interest readings about fascinating people and places.

GOLDEN DOOR

(PAGES 3–13)

Pre-Reading Activities

Discussion Questions

1. About statues: What is a statue? Statues are often built to honor a person or an event. What famous statues can you name?

2. About students' familiarity with Liberty: Have you ever heard of the Statue of Liberty? What do you know about it? Where is it? Can you guess its height? Who gave it to the United States?

3. About treatment of new immigrants: Why is any government careful about who enters the country? What kinds of people do they want to keep out? How are visitors and immigrants screened?

4. About geography: Why were most of the immigrants who came to Ellis Island from Europe? Where do you think Asian arrivals entered the country?

5. About Liberty's appearance: What's in each hand? What is on her head? What does her robe remind you of? What kind of shoes is she wearing? What is around her feet? Does she look typically American? What aspects of the statue's style show the influence of classical antiquity?

6. About the chapter title: This selection is about two different but closely related sites: the Statue of Liberty and Ellis Island. How does each site relate to the chapter title? What is the golden door?

7. About the teaser: Where do you think the Statue of Liberty came from? Did the United States create it, or was it a gift from another country? (Paragraphs 12 and 13 provide the answer to the teaser.)

Section Headings

"A $70 Million Face-Lift": Ask students if they think the heading means that something was done to Liberty's face.

"The French Connection": Ask students what movie this subhead refers to.

"What She Stands For": Ask students what pun is involved in this subhead.

"Coming to America": Ask students what movie this heading refers to.

Important Vocabulary from the Reading

1. Introduce the following pairs of words, and be sure that students are able to distinguish between them: *sculpture* and *sculptor*; *sculpture* and *statue*; *sculpture* and *architecture*; *repair* and *restore*.

2. Discuss words and phrases related to getting money for good causes, such as *donate*, *donation*, and *donor*; *contribute* and *contribution*; and *to raise money*.

3. Discuss the meaning of *irony* and the adjective *ironic*. Have students then look for examples in the text and in their own lives.

Activities to Accompany the Reading

Playing Word Games

To practice nouns, especially occupations, Who Does It? is a good game. In this game, the questions must relate to the vocabulary in the reading. Here are some sample questions: Who comes to a new country to live permanently? (an immigrant) Who designs buildings? (an architect) Who designs statues? (a sculptor) Who gives money to charity? (a donor, a contributor) Who poses for a statue? (a model) Prepare the questions and put them on separate cards or on a sheet of paper, or have students scan the reading and help write the questions. Play the game with teams of two or with small groups.

Improvising Scenes

1. Have students create the scene in which Bartholdi asks his mother to be his model for the Statue of Liberty's face.

2. Ask students to pretend that they are standing on Liberty Island and having a conversation about the statue.

3. Have students pretend to be immigrants who have just landed on Ellis Island. Have them talk about their plans, hopes, and fears.

Summarizing the Text

Have students tell how to get to Liberty Island and the top of the Statue of Liberty.

Using Maps

Have students look at a map of New York City and find the ocean, harbor, boroughs, and other sites.

Studying Word Parts to Build Vocabulary

The word *pedestal* contains the word part *ped-*, which can mean "foot" or "child." Ask students to think of other words they know with *ped-* in them (*pedal, pediatrician,* etc.) and tell what the words mean. Have them also list words with *cent-*.

Reviewing Roman Numerals

The date on the statue's tablet is written in Roman numerals: July IV, MDCCLXXVI. Show students how to read that as July 4, 1776.

Discussion, Writing, or Research Topics

1. Ask for students' reactions to the Statue of Liberty. Ask them the following: Do you like it? What attitudes do you see in the facial expression?

2. Ask students these questions: If the Statue of Liberty were alive, what would she think of the nation or the world that she sees today? Is liberty enlightening the world now?

3. Compare and contrast the two most well-known symbols of the United States, the Statue of Liberty and Uncle Sam.

4. Note the classical elements in the statue. These include the crown, robe, sandals, and Roman numerals. Bartholdi was greatly influenced by the ancient Greek and Roman cultures. The crown is reminiscent of medieval religious paintings.

Extension Activities

1. Read and discuss "The New Colossus," by Emma Lazarus. This poem is a sonnet, so use this opportunity to introduce students to the sonnet form. Show some drawings of the Colossus of Rhodes, which the Statue of Liberty is compared to in the sonnet. The Colossus of Rhodes was one of the Seven Wonders of the Ancient World. Information about it and drawings of it can be found in most encyclopedias.

2. Take students on a tour of your town to look at some of its sculpture. Compare some modern sculpture to the Statue of Liberty and other 19th-century statues.

For ESL Students

1. This reading contains several past participles as adjectives, so this is a good time to teach the differences between the present participle and past participle as adjectives. Some common pairs that ESL students often confuse are *boring* and *bored*; *exciting* and *excited*; and *interesting* and *interested*. Begin with these common words. Then work on the pairs that have at least one of the words in the reading (*exhausting* and *exhausted*; *confusing* and *confused*; *embarrassing* and *embarrassed*; etc.). The exercises in this guide provide some practice with these forms, but some students may need additional help.

2. This reading contains the phrasal verb *let go*. Be sure that ESL students do not confuse it with *let's go*.

READING COMPREHENSION

A. Mark each of these statements *True* or *False*.

_____ 1. The Statue of Liberty symbolizes the power of the American government.

_____ 2. There isn't a real flame in the statue's torch.

_____ 3. The Statue of Liberty has been standing on Ellis Island for more than 100 years.

_____ 4. Some Ellis Island arrivals were sent back home.

_____ 5. The word *restore* means to return something to a store.

B. The words *and*, *but*, *or*, and *so* are sometimes used to show the relationship between two ideas. Use one of them to connect the ideas in these sentences.

1. Bartholdi came to the United States, _____ he sold the idea of the Statue of Liberty to important Americans.

2. Bartholdi designed the exterior of the statue, _____ he didn't design the interior.

3. The Americans were supposed to build the pedestal, _____ they didn't have enough money.

4. You can take the elevator to the base of the statue, _____ you can walk up the stairs.

5. I don't want to walk up so many stairs, _____ I'm going to take the elevator.

C. Answer the following questions. Write complete sentences.

1. How tall is the Statue of Liberty without its pedestal?

_____

2. Who designed the inside (the "skeleton" or framework) of Liberty?

_____

3. Where is Ellis Island?

_____

4. Who goes to Ellis Island today?

_____

VOCABULARY PRACTICE

A. Use some of these words to complete the sentences that follow.

deported	famous	pedestal	symbol
donated	overthrow	popular	tyranny

1. He's not a very _____ president. I don't think he will be reelected.

2. Many people emigrate from their native country because of the _____ of an evil government.

3. The American flag is a _____ of the United States.

4. It is illegal to try to _____ the government.

5. New arrivals to the United States were _____ if they were mentally ill or criminals.

B. Circle the word that best completes each sentence.

1. I'm very tired. In fact, I'm (embarrassed, exhausted, enthusiastic, exhausting).

2. In 1886, American women recognized the (iron, irony, enthusiasm, tyranny) of a woman symbolizing freedom.

3. He thinks his father is the smartest, most wonderful man in the world. He puts him on a (harbor, pedestal, torch, project).

4. About $140 million was spent on the Ellis Island (communication, immigration, restoration, transportation).

5. He (deported, donated, declared, designed) $500 to his church.

6. My (favorite, famous, popular, enormous) color is red.

7. Ships go in and out of a (monument, pedestal, harbor, torch).

8. The Statue of Liberty is very big. In fact, it's (popular, exhausting, enthusiastic, colossal).

ATTRACTIONS *Teacher's Guide*
© 1994 Contemporary Books
A Reproducible Exercise Page

HOMONYMS, SYNONYMS, AND SIMILAR WORDS

A. Say these homonyms aloud. Then use them to complete the sentences that follow.

I'll = I will   *isle* = a small island   *aisle* = a path or row

1. Liberty Island is small. It could be called an _____.

2. Walk down the second _____ to get to your seats.

3. In which _____ will I find the canned soups?

4. When I get back from my vacation, _____ call you.

B. Match each word in the column on the left with the correct word or phrase in the column on the right. Write the correct letters on the blank lines.

_____ **1.** donate

_____ **2.** enthusiasm

_____ **3.** pedestal

_____ **4.** site

_____ **5.** spike

_____ **6.** story

(a) great interest in something

(b) a floor of a building; a narrative

(c) place, location

(d) something to stand on

(e) something thin and pointed, usually metal

(f) give away to a good cause

PARTS OF SPEECH AND INFLECTED FORMS

Sometimes past participles of verbs are used as adjectives.

Examples: the *broken* chain, her *raised* hand (11)

A. Make phrases with these past participles by adding a noun.

a torn _____   an embarrassed _____

a damaged _____   a frightened _____

B. Put *a/an* and a past participle in front of these nouns.

Examples: *a lighted* torch, a *frozen* cake

_____ book   _____ elevator

_____ immigrant   _____ word

WORD PARTS

Study the meanings of these word parts from the reading. Then use them to complete the words in the sentences that follow.

cent- = one hundred   *gigant-* = large   *port-* = carry
-cide = killer, killing   *mis-* = bad(ly), wrong(ly)   *spec-* = see
de- = away from, down   *ped(o)-* = foot, child

1. When you drive a car, you put your feet on the _____als.

2. That man killed himself. He committed sui_____.

3. The government sent that immigrant back to his native country. He was _____ported because of past criminal activities.

4. The doctor in_____ted the patient's injury carefully.

5. Various vehicles of trans_____ation carry a person across land, sea, or air.

6. The Statue of Liberty is often described as _____ic or enormous because it is 151 feet tall.

7. The Statue of Liberty stands on a ten-story _____estal.

8. The _____ennial celebration of Liberty was in 1986. That was the statue's 100th birthday.

9. The homi_____ rate for the city is very high. A lot of people get killed here.

10. Drivers must always yield to _____estrians.

11. When you _____spell a word, you make a _____take.

12. You have to ascend and _____scend the statue on foot.

ATTRACTIONS *Teacher's Guide*
© 1994 Contemporary Books
A Reproducible Exercise Page

PHRASAL VERBS AND OTHER IDIOMS

A. Circle the correct answers.

   1. In paragraph 7, <u>sell the idea</u> means (a) get people to support it (b) get cash for it.

   2. In paragraph 8, <u>raised the $400,000</u> means (a) lifted it (b) got people to donate it.

   3. In paragraph 24, <u>the old country</u> means (a) an immigrant's native country (b) a country that's at least 500 years old.

B. Reread the paragraphs that these phrasal verbs are used in. The paragraph numbers are in parentheses. Then use the phrasal verbs to complete the sentences that follow. Note that some phrasal verbs can be separated. A noun or a pronoun can come between the two parts of the verb.

stands for (11)	put together (15)	clean up (23)
take apart (15)	let go (19)	fix up (23)

   1. Hold my hand now. After we cross the street, you can _____ of my hand.

   2. Please don't take the clock apart. I don't know how to _____ it _____ again.

   3. The kitchen is very messy. Let's _____ it _____.

   4. The Statue of Liberty is a symbol. It _____ freedom and opportunity.

   5. There are a lot of mistakes in this composition. Rewrite it and _____ it _____.

   6. Why did the French have to _____ the Statue of Liberty before shipping it to the United States?

PATTERN PRACTICE

A. Circle the word that best completes each sentence. (Choose the present or past participle.)

1. It's (embarrassing, embarrassed) to forget someone's name.

2. I was (exhausting, exhausted) after I ran five miles.

3. I didn't understand the directions. I was (confused, confusing).

4. Playing tennis all day is (exhausting, exhausted).

B. Complete these sentences.

1. I was very excited about _____.

2. It is exhausting to _____.

3. I feel embarrassed when I _____.

4. I'm enthusiastic about _____.

PHONICS AND PRONUNCIATION

A. The letter _g_ has two sounds. The soft _g_ (as in _gentle_) usually comes before _e, i,_ or _y_. The hard _g_ (as in _gun_) comes before all other letters. But some words don't follow the rule.

How many soft _g_s are in these words? _____ Circle them.

agreement	courage	generous	gigantic	guest
baggage	damage	gift	granite	language

B. Read these words aloud. All of them have the sound _zh_. There is no English letter for this sound. Circle the letter(s) that make the sound _zh_ in each word below.

garage   pleasure   version   measure   television   usually

ATTRACTIONS *Teacher's Guide*
© 1994 Contemporary Books
A Reproducible Exercise Page

SKY HIGH

(PAGES 17–25)

Pre-Reading Activities

Discussion Questions

1. About skyscrapers: What is a skyscraper? How tall are they? Have you ever seen one? Did you travel to the top? How was the view? What's the difference between a high-rise and a skyscraper? Why do some high-rises have no 13th floor? Do you know about skyscrapers now under construction that will be taller than Sears Tower? (A pair of 1,476-foot towers are being built in Malaysia. When completed in 1996, they will be 22 feet taller than Sears Tower.)

2. About students' attitudes toward skyscrapers: Do you like them? Would it frighten you to work or live in one? What are some things that people might be afraid of when they are inside a skyscraper? What are some things that might be annoying or uncomfortable about living or working in a skyscraper?

3. About Spider-Man: The character called Spider-Man appears in comic books, comic strips, and cartoons. What do you know about him? Is he a good guy or a bad guy? What does he do? What special abilities does he have? What does he wear? What traits does he share with a spider? (Show students a Spider-Man comic.)

4. About Sears, Roebuck and Co.: What type of business is it? What other companies are similar? Are there any Sears retail stores in your town or city? Did you ever buy anything from a mail-order catalog, either Sears's or another company's?

5. About the teaser: What does the word *universe* mean? Is it possible for the universe to be inside Sears Tower? If not, can you guess the answer to the question? (Paragraph 13 provides the answer to the teaser.)

Section Headings

"Reaching the Top—The Hard Way": Discuss its meaning in the business world.

Important Vocabulary from the Reading

1. Have students scan the reading for compound words and phrases beginning with *sky*. In addition to *skyscraper*, they'll find *skydeck* and *skylobby*. Discuss the meanings of these words. Then ask students to brainstorm with a partner and try to think of more compound words that begin with sky (*skylight, skyline, skywriter,* etc.).

2. Discuss *challenge* and *compromise*. Have students give examples of these words to be sure the meaning is clear.

3. Discuss the two meanings of *story* (a narrative and a floor of a building).

4. Pronounce and discuss the word pairs *costume* and *custom, sculpture* and *architecture*.

Activities to Accompany the Reading

Playing Word Games

Have students work in groups of three to list, without using the text or a dictionary, compound words (either hyphenated or written as one word) beginning with *s*. Their words don't have to be from the reading. Allow about three minutes. Then have each group put its list on the board. Read the words aloud, correct the spelling, and then determine the winning team.

Improvising Scenes

Have students perform the action in the first section, with people playing the roles of Spider Dan, the Sears employee who called the police, the firefighters who tried to persuade him to stop climbing, and various spectators making appropriate comments.

Summarizing the Text

After reading the first section, have students summarize the action orally or in writing.

Using Maps

On a map of the United States, have students find Chicago and discuss why a large city developed in this location. Have them locate the surrounding states that can sometimes be seen from the top of Sears Tower: Indiana, Michigan, and Wisconsin. On a map of Chicago, have the students find Lake Michigan, the Chicago River, and particular sites mentioned in the reading.

Studying Word Parts to Build Vocabulary

1. Point out that the negative prefix *il-* is used before words beginning with *l.* Discuss the meanings of *illegible* and *illegitimate.* Be sure that students don't confuse *il-* with *ill-*, which means "bad(ly)" or "poor(ly)," as in *ill-advised.*

2. To teach *uni-*, meaning "one," ask what a unicycle is and what United States means.

Reading for Details

Ask students to read the section titled "Amazing Facts About the Sears Tower" and try to remember some of the important statistical details. Then have them close the book. Ask what kinds of facts were given (height, weight, speed of the elevator, etc.). Then see how close they can get to giving the correct figures.

Doing Related Math

The size of Sears Tower seems even more amazing when you and your class change the tons to pounds and the feet to inches. Also, convert nonmetric measurements to metric.

Other Visual Aids

Show photographs of Sears Tower and other Chicago landmarks mentioned in the reading, such as Buckingham Fountain.

Studying the Calder Sculpture

Look carefully at the photograph of *Universe* and identify the various parts: spiral, spine, flowers, sun, and pendulum. Point out that the pendulum symbolizes the passage of time.

Discussion, Writing, or Research Topics

Have students select one of the following topics, do library research on their topic, and then work with classmates to prepare a group presentation for the class.

- the construction of skyscrapers
- the World Trade Center bombing (March 1993)
- the Great Chicago Fire (1871)
- the history of Sears, Roebuck and Co.
- the mobiles of Alexander Calder

Extension Activities

1. Have the class watch parts of movies that have scenes occurring in or on skyscrapers. Two possibilities are *King Kong*, which concludes at the Empire State Building, and *The Towering Inferno*, about a fire in a skyscraper.

2. Take students on a field trip to a nearby skyscraper or to an art museum that features works by Calder.

For ESL Students

Some ESL students are not familiar with nonmetric measurements, so it is important to explain them. Show the class a 12-inch ruler and a yardstick with inches on one side and centimeters on the other. Have students compare the inch to the centimeter and the foot and yard to the meter. Review the nonmetric measurements for length, and have students convert them to metric. Teach the ounce and the pound by weighing some things on a small scale. Explain the difference between a ton in American measurements and a metric ton.

READING COMPREHENSION

A. Mark each of these statements *True* or *False*.

_____ **1.** Spider Dan was climbing Sears Tower to wash the windows.

_____ **2.** A building must be 50 stories high to be called a skyscraper.

_____ **3.** Sears, Roebuck and Co. uses very little of the office space in Sears Tower.

_____ **4.** Mrs. O'Leary and her cow died in the Great Chicago Fire of 1871.

_____ **5.** During the Great Chicago Fire, many of the city's skyscrapers burned down.

_____ **6.** The tallest building in Chicago is one mile high.

B. What does each word mean in the paragraph indicated? Reread the paragraphs, and circle the letter of the correct answer.

1. cling (2): (a) make a loud noise (b) hold onto very tightly

2. avoid (3): (a) reach (b) get away from

3. compromise (4): (a) an agreement in which each side partially gives in to the wishes of the other side (b) an agreement in which one side completely gives in to the wishes of the other side

4. boasts (7): (a) brags (b) explains

5. sways (14): (a) moves up and down (b) moves from side to side

6. address (15): (a) speaking (b) a specific location

7. threat (16): (a) danger (b) support

8. drawn (20): (a) sketched in a picture (b) attracted

9. limit (23): (a) a short amount of time (b) as far as it's possible to go, the ending point

10. architect (23): (a) designer of buildings (b) designer of sculpture

READING COMPREHENSION (CONTINUED)

C. Reread each paragraph indicated. Then write a question that the paragraph answers. Then write the answer.

1. Paragraph 3:

Where _____?

_____

2. Paragraph 10:

When _____?

_____

3. Paragraph 19:

What _____?

_____

D. Mark each statement *F* if it is a fact and *O* if it is an opinion.

_____ **1.** Dan Goodwin is a brave man.

_____ **2.** Sears Tower is the tallest building in Chicago.

_____ **3.** Calder's sculpture *Universe* moves.

_____ **4.** There is no limit to the height of a skyscraper.

E. Complete these statements.

1. Some people are afraid to work in a skyscraper because _____

_____.

2. Dan Goodwin will probably not climb Sears Tower again because _____

_____.

3. A lot of tourists come to Sears Tower every day because _____

_____.

ATTRACTIONS *Teacher's Guide*
© 1994 Contemporary Books
A Reproducible Exercise Page

VOCABULARY PRACTICE

A. Say these vocabulary words aloud. Then use some of them to complete the sentences that follow.

approaching	level	spectators
automatic	limit	survived
avoid	pendulum	trespassing

1. The car was _____ me very fast, so I jumped back on the sidewalk to _____ it.

2. The man was driving 20 miles above the speed _____.

3. We couldn't go on that beautiful beach because a sign said, "Private property. No _____."

4. Every skyscraper has _____ elevators.

5. Spider Dan didn't fall off Sears Tower. He _____ the climb.

B. Use some of these compound words to complete the sentences that follow.

fireproof	high-speed	strange-looking
headquarters	skyscrapers	wind-resistant
heavyweight	skydeck	world-famous

1. Sears Tower is well protected against fire because it was built with _____ steel.

2. The spectators saw a man in a _____ costume climbing Sears Tower.

3. A _____ engineer named Fazlur Khan helped to design Sears Tower.

4. He gave it a very _____ structure.

5. We drove along Lake Michigan and looked at the skyline of Chicago with its many _____.

6. Sears, Roebuck and Co. no longer has its _____ in Sears Tower.

HOMONYMS, SYNONYMS, AND SIMILAR WORDS

These word pairs are homonyms. (They sound the same.)

higher / hire   waist / waste

These words are not homonyms, but they are easy to confuse because they sound very similar or are spelled with many of the same letters:

quit / quite / quiet   high / height

The word *story* has two meanings: a narrative tale and one floor of a building. Say the homonyms and similar words above aloud. Then use some of them to complete these sentences.

1. Don't _____ time. It is the most valuable thing you have.

2. He wore a belt around his _____.

3. Did you _____ someone to fix the roof?

4. What is the _____ of Sears Tower? It's 1,454 feet tall.

5. He _____ his job because he didn't like his boss.

6. In a library, you should always be _____.

7. The movie wasn't _____ as good as I had expected it to be.

8. I live in a three-_____ building.

9. This _____ about Spider Dan is true.

PARTS OF SPEECH AND INFLECTED FORMS

The endings *-er* and *-or* are sometimes used in words that name the person or thing that does a job. Complete these sentences with an appropriate noun that ends in *-er* or *-or*.

1. He climbs mountains. He's a mountain _____.

2. It generates electricity. It's a _____.

3. It sprinkles water on a fire or on grass. It's a _____.

4. It's a high-rise that seems to scrape the sky. It's a _____.

5. She's visiting Chicago. She's a _____ here.

ATTRACTIONS *Teacher's Guide*
© 1994 Contemporary Books
A Reproducible Exercise Page

WORD PARTS

What do these word parts mean?

1. *auto-* in *automatic?* _____

2. *il-* in *illegal?* _____

3. *uni-* in *universe?* _____

PHRASAL VERBS AND OTHER IDIOMS

A. **Reread the paragraphs that the idioms in the column on the left are used in. Then match each idiom with its definition in the column on the right. Write the correct letters on the blank lines.**

_____ **1.** give up (3)   **(a)** alternate

_____ **2.** talk into (3)   **(b)** stop, quit

_____ **3.** get trapped (15)   **(c)** persuade, convince

_____ **4.** take turns (23)   **(d)** be unable to escape

B. **Now write sentences about the following phrases.**

1. something you gave up _____

_____

2. something you once talked someone into doing _____

_____

3. something you and a friend took turns doing _____

_____

4. a time when you got trapped in a place _____

_____

PATTERN PRACTICE

Special endings are used when we are comparing two or more things. Complete these statements using *the/than* and by adding *-er* or *-est* to the adjective written after each sentence. Change the spelling of the adjectives that end in *y*.

1. Sears Tower is _____ _____ building in the world. (tall)

2. The John Hancock Center was completed in 1968. It is _____ _____ Sears Tower. (old)

3. The Hancock Building has _____ _____ elevator in the world. It's even _____ _____ the ones in Sears Tower. (fast)

4. A meter is _____ _____ a foot. (long)

5. A ton is _____ _____ a pound. (heavy)

6. Chicago's O'Hare Airport is _____ _____ in the world. (busy)

PHONICS AND PRONUNCIATION

A. Say these pairs of words aloud. Then circle the pairs that rhyme.

light / right	climb / crime
lies / rise	floor / forest
flames / frames	pilot / private

B. Answer these questions using ordinal numbers. Write the answers, and say them aloud. Be careful to pronounce the *th* sounds correctly.

1. On what date did Goodwin climb Sears Tower? _____

2. What floor did Goodwin reach at 6:10 A.M.? _____

3. What floor was he on when he stopped climbing? _____

4. In Sears Tower, what floor is the skydeck on? _____

5. Is the Hancock Center the second tallest skyscraper in the world? No, it's the _____.

ATTRACTIONS *Teacher's Guide*
© 1994 Contemporary Books
A Reproducible Exercise Page

GATEWAY TO THE WEST

(PAGES 29–39)

Pre-Reading Activities

Discussion Questions

1. About arches: What is an arch? What famous arches have you heard of? What kinds of structures sometimes have arches? How old do you think the arch as an architectural form is? Who do you think were the first people to build it?

2. About the Gateway Arch: Do you like the design? How tall would you guess it is? Would you like to go to the top? Do you think it's possible? How?

3. About westward expansion: When was the western part of the United States developed? What different groups of people helped to develop it? What inventions helped to develop it?

4. About adages: Have you heard the sayings "Like father, like son" and "The apple doesn't fall far from the tree"? Do you agree with them? Can you think of some famous people who took after a famous parent?

5. About the teaser: Is the Gateway Arch taller than it is wide or vice versa? What do you think? (The answer is in paragraph 8.)

Section Headings

Ask students the following questions regarding headings and subheads:

"Arch of Triumph": What is a triumph? Why could Saarinen's arch be described as a triumph? Where else is there an Arch of Triumph? (The Arc de Triomphe is in Paris, France.)

"Impressive Facts": What kinds of facts about the Arch would they expect to find in this section?

"A Hidden Museum": Where could a museum be hidden?

"A $15 Million Bargain": What is a bargain? Would someone paying $15 million for something consider it a bargain?

"The Lewis and Clark Expedition": Have you ever heard of Lewis and Clark? Do you know why they're famous?

"Westward Ho!": In the 19th century, who went west and why?

"The Last Frontier": What is a frontier? Why is the West called the last frontier? Is it really? What about space exploration?

Important Vocabulary from the Reading

1. Before they begin to read, be sure that students understand the following words: *gateway, arch, expansion,* and the related words *deceive, deceiving, deceptive,* and *deception.*

2. Show pictures of some of the wild animals mentioned in the reading, especially the beaver, grizzly bear, ox, bison, and prairie dog.

Activities to Accompany the Reading

Playing Word Games

Have students work in pairs to make a list of antonyms with words from this reading. Then use their lists to create a timed antonym game to be played competitively with partners.

Improvising Scenes

1. Have students act out a scene in which Saarinen explains to the people who gave him the prize that as designed, his monument won't stand up.

2. Have students act as members of the Lewis and Clark expedition returning from their trip and describing their discoveries.

Summarizing the Text

Have students summarize the events surrounding the contest for the memorial.

Using Maps

Point out to students the major sections of the United States. Be sure they know the area called the Great Plains and understand what the name tells about the land. Have students point out the following places and bodies of water mentioned in the reading: St. Louis, the Mississippi River, the Missouri River, the Louisiana Territory, Oregon, and the Pacific Ocean.

Studying Word Parts to Build Vocabulary

List words that have the word part *ex-*. Then note the different meanings of *ex-*, and group the words by these meanings.

Discussion, Writing, or Research Topics

Have students answer these questions:

1. Does the West still attract Americans? Would you want to live in the West? If so, what state would you move to? Why? What frontiers lie ahead for tomorrow's explorers to "tame"?

2. This selection touched upon a great wealth of very interesting historic topics. Have students work in groups to research these topics and then tell the class more about them. The following interesting topics are suggested:

   • other works of Eero Saarinen
   • Thomas Jefferson, an architect and a statesman
   • the Lewis and Clark expedition
   • plants and animals of the West (cactus, bison, etc.)
   • St. Louis—what is it like today?
   • heroes and/or villains of the Wild West
   • how cowboys really lived
   • movies about the West

Extension Activities

1. Have students read about the different styles and shapes of arches in an encyclopedia or art book and then look around their neighborhoods for arches used in buildings, bridges, etc. They might sketch or photograph them and present their findings to the class.

2. Have students pretend to be modern-day explorers of the West. Ask students how they would get to the West Coast by train or car starting out from St. Louis or from their present place of residence. Have them get routes from railroad companies or plan car routes by studying road maps. Computer programs are another source of travel information. Then have them write out their routes.

3. Have students fill in maps of the United States with the following information:

   • the years in which various areas became U.S. land (Have them color each acquisition a different color.)
   • the Lewis and Clark Expedition routes to and from St. Louis (Have students trace the routes on the map.)

4. Show a Western film or part of one. Ask students to note the lifestyle and the values depicted.

For ESL Students

1. Discuss the use of a saying in paragraph 6: ". . . a structure that could stand firmly on its own two legs." It's a variation of "He can stand on his own two feet," which describes an independent person.

2. Clarify measurements. Be sure that students understand how long a mile is. Compare it to a kilometer.

3. Discuss the differences between *slender* and *narrow*. Point out that *narrow* is not used to describe a person's figure. Contrast *slender* (which has a positive connotation) with *skinny* (which has a negative connotation).

4. Ask students to name some things that can stretch. Demonstrate stretching with a rubber band and/or a piece of elastic. Discuss the following expressions: stretch out your arms, stretch your dollars, stretch the truth, stretch the Constitution.

READING COMPREHENSION

A. Mark each of these statements *True* or *False*.

_____ 1. The Gateway Arch honors the people who developed the American West.

_____ 2. The Gateway Arch is the tallest structure in the world.

_____ 3. Trams run up and down the inside of the Arch.

_____ 4. The United States got most of the West by buying land and by winning a war.

_____ 5. The Louisiana Territory was about the size of the state of Louisiana.

B. Answer these questions about the reading. Write complete sentences.

1. What is the outside of the Gateway Arch made of?

_____

2. Where is the Arch's observation room?

_____

3. Where is the Museum of Westward Expansion?

_____

4. Why did people go west in the 19th century?

_____

5. How did the American West change between 1800 and 1890?

_____

6. What harm did westward expansion do?

_____

7. Why was the memorial to westward expansion named in honor of Thomas Jefferson?

_____

VOCABULARY PRACTICE

A. **Say these words aloud, and discuss their meanings. Then use some of them to complete the sentences that follow.**

arch	expansion	gateway	stretch
deceived	fragile	plains	tame
doubled	frontier	slender	wilderness

1. Flat areas (without hills or mountains) are called _____.

2. When the United States purchased the Louisiana Territory, the country _____ in size.

3. Many dangerous animals, such as grizzly bears, lived in the _____ of the Old West.

4. A prairie dog is a wild animal. My dog is very _____.

5. The word _____ means the boundary where settled areas end and wilderness begins.

6. New York Harbor was the _____ to the United States for immigrants coming from Europe.

7. An _____ is a curved structure.

8. Don't trust a person who _____ you in the past.

9. If you _____ a rubber band, it expands (gets bigger).

10. Don't sit on that chair. It's _____, and it may break.

B. **Match each word in the column on the left with its opposite in the column on the right. Write the correct letters on the blank lines.**

_____ 1. eventually   **(a)** friendly

_____ 2. curved   **(b)** wide

_____ 3. hostile   **(c)** tame

_____ 4. slender   **(d)** straight

_____ 5. wild   **(e)** immediately, right away

ATTRACTIONS *Teacher's Guide*
© 1994 Contemporary Books
A Reproducible Exercise Page

HOMONYMS, SYNONYMS, AND SIMILAR WORDS

These word pairs are homonyms. (They sound the same.)

heard / herd

plain (adjective) and plain (noun) / plane

miner / minor

new / knew

Say the homonyms above aloud, and then use them to complete these sentences.

1. Our _____ took off and landed on time.

2. Have your ever _____ a _____ of bison running across a _____? They make a lot of noise!

3. There isn't any decoration on this cake. It's very _____.

4. A coal _____ works underground.

5. A _____ is a person who is not an adult.

6. The _____ student in class _____ all the answers.

PARTS OF SPEECH AND INFLECTED FORMS

A. Write the noun form of each adjective:

1. deep _____ **2.** high _____ **3.** long _____ **4.** wide _____

B. Use the eight words from Part A to complete these sentences.

1. How _____ does a big airplane usually fly?

2. How big is this desk? What are its dimensions, its _____, _____, and _____?

3. In one place, the Pacific Ocean is 36,198 feet _____.

4. The _____ and _____ of the Gateway Arch are the same.

5. A yard isn't as _____ as a meter.

6. A river isn't as _____ as an ocean.

WORD PARTS

Study the meanings of these word parts from the reading. Then use some of them to complete the words in the sentences that follow.

> *ex-* = from, out, away from, not having, former
> *expan-* = a spreading out
> *habit-* = to live in or occupy
> *-less* = without, lacking, not capable of being
> *-ward* = moving in a certain direction

1. The bison almost became ____tinct because of west_____ expansion.

2. Native Americans and wild animals in_____ed the West before the European explorers and settlers arrived.

3. I saw a car coming to_____ me very fast. I jumped out of its way.

4. ____plorers went into unsettled areas away from the towns.

5. Stain_____ steel will not rust or get permanent stains on it.

PHRASAL VERBS AND OTHER IDIOMS

Reread the paragraphs that these idioms are used in. The paragraph numbers are given in parentheses. Then use the idioms to complete the sentences that follow.

> trick the eye (8)   round-trip (21)
> get out (12)   roundup (28)

1. Let's _____ and enjoy the nice weather today.

2. After a _____ of all the children, the teacher took attendance.

3. We can't buy a _____ ticket on the bus; we can buy only a one-way ticket.

4. The saying "seeing is believing" isn't a very good one. Some things _____.

ATTRACTIONS *Teacher's Guide*
© 1994 Contemporary Books
A Reproducible Exercise Page

PATTERN PRACTICE

A. Read the paragraphs indicated in the parentheses. Then use an appropriate past-tense verb to complete these sentences.

1. A competition _____ _____ to select a design for a memorial to westward expansion. (1)

2. Construction _____ _____ because of a lack of funds. (6)

3. The Arch _____ _____ to withstand strong winds and earthquakes. (11)

4. In 1800, the land west of the Mississippi River _____ _____ by other countries. (15)

5. The land that Jefferson bought from Napoleon _____ _____ the Louisiana Territory. (17)

6. In 1872, barbed wire _____ _____. (28)

B. Study the difference between *its* and *it's*.

> *its* = belonging to something, a part of something (a possessive adjective)
> *it's* = it is (a pronoun + a verb)

Use *its* or *it's* correctly in each sentence. Be sure to capitalize the first letter of a word beginning a sentence.

1. _____ the tallest arch in the world.

2. _____ height is 630 feet.

3. _____ slender and graceful.

4. _____ outside layer is polished stainless steel.

5. A museum is hidden underground between _____ legs.

PHONICS AND PRONUNCIATION

**A. Practice the sounds *s* and *sh* by reading these pairs of words aloud.
Circle the *sh* sounds.**

save / shave	scrape / shape	machine / matching
sell / shell	sign / shine	sir / sure

**B. All English vowels have more than one sound. When the letter sounds the same as its
name, that is the long vowel sound. The other common vowel sound is the short
vowel sound. Read these words aloud. Then complete the chart by writing in
additional words with each vowel's long and short sounds.**

	Long Vowel	Short Vowel		Long Vowel	Short Vowel
a	train	tram	a	_____	_____
e	deep	depth	e	_____	_____
i	wild	wilderness	i	_____	_____
	wide	width		_____	_____
o	cope	continent	o	_____	_____
u	music	must	u	_____	_____

**C. Discuss the letter combinations that usually make a long vowel sound. Which of these
words has a long vowel sound?**

still   steel

_____

**D. The letter combination *ei* may be pronounced as long *a*, long *e*, or long *i*. Say these
words aloud: *deceive*, *eight*, and *height*. Now put each word after the correct vowel
sound.**

long *a* _____ long *e* _____ long *i* _____

ATTRACTIONS *Teacher's Guide*
© 1994 Contemporary Books
A Reproducible Exercise Page

HEADS OF STATE

(PAGES 43–53)

Pre-Reading Activities

Discussion Questions

1. About Mount Rushmore: Where is Mount Rushmore? What presidents are represented? What information about the heads do you expect to find in this reading? (Make a list of student predictions on the board. Later, check to see if the reading matched the predictions.)

2. About American Indians: What do you know about the American government's past and present treatment of Indians? How have American attitudes toward Indians changed in the past 50 years or so? Do you know any Indians? What are their attitudes and problems? Do they prefer to be called American Indians or Native Americans?

3. About Indian heroes: What Native American heroes, male or female, have you heard of? What do you know about Sitting Bull or Crazy Horse?

4. About mountain carving: How do you think it's done? What equipment is needed? What dangers are involved?

5. About the chapter title: What does "Heads of State" mean? (Discuss the chapter title's literal and figurative meanings. Define the word *pun*.) How many different sites are included? What are they? (There are two: Mount Rushmore and the Crazy Horse Memorial.)

6. About the teaser: (The answer to the first part of the teaser, 465 feet, is on the Sidelights page. The answer to the second part is in paragraph 10. Each head is about as tall as a five-story building.)

Section Headings

"Crazy Horse Rides Again": Ask students what the heading brings to mind. Older students and fans of old-time radio may recall the famous words, "The Lone Ranger rides again!"

Important Vocabulary from the Reading

1. The word *monument* comes from a Latin verb meaning "remind" or "warn." Ask students what monuments they know of that serve each of these purposes. Also, point out that the word *monumental* usually means "massive" or "very large."

2. Some geological terms to introduce before students tackle the reading are *granite*, *hills*, *peaks*, *slopes*, *mountain ranges*, and *plains*. The Sidelights page includes the words *badlands*, *gullies*, and *glaciers*. If possible, show photos of these formations.

Activities to Accompany the Reading

Playing Word Games

1. Have students work in pairs to try to make as many new words as possible by adding prefixes and/or suffixes to the words below. Set a time limit, and score the papers with the class.

agree	create	important	orphan
art	design	known	quick
big	easy	lead	spirit
carve	great	measure	symbol
cell	honor	nation	union

2. Have students write all the words they can think of that mean "very big."

Improvising Scenes

1. Have students improvise the scene that tells how Mount Rushmore got its name.

2. Have students improvise the deathbed scene with Ziolkowski and his wife and ten children.

3. Have students improvise the scene in which Crazy Horse is murdered.

Comparing and Contrasting

Have students compare and contrast the two sculptures described in this chapter. List similarities on the board in one column and differences in another.

Using Maps

1. Have students find South Dakota on a map of the United States. Then have them locate Keystone and Rapid City. Mount Rushmore is about 25 miles southwest of Rapid City and 3 miles from Keystone. Have students find Castle Rock, the geographical center of the country, and the Black Hills. Note what states they are in.

2. On a map of the world or of North and South America, have students find the Panama Canal. Discuss its importance.

Discussion, Writing, or Research Topics

1. Discuss these two quotations from the reading: "I'm making Roosevelt's glasses out of the most precious thing on earth: imagination." "Every man has his mountain. I'm carving mine."

2. Divide the class into small groups to research the people listed below in the library and report to the class a few facts about them that they think the class may not know.

George Washington	Gutzon Borglum
Thomas Jefferson	Crazy Horse
Abraham Lincoln	Calamity Jane
Theodore Roosevelt	Wild Bill Hickok

Extension Activities

Show a videotape about the Crazy Horse Memorial. To purchase an 85-minute videotape about the memorial, write or phone Crazy Horse, Avenue of the Chiefs, The Black Hills, Crazy Horse, SD 57730-9506, (605) 673-4681.

For ESL Students

1. Have students look at a map of the United States and practice talking about directions. Remind them that when combining two directions, *north* or *south* goes before *east* or *west*. For example, New York City is *northeast* of Los Angeles. Then ask students what directions they would travel on the following trips:

- from Rapid City, South Dakota, to Cheyenne, Wyoming
- from Texas to Oregon
- from Seattle, Washington, to Washington, D.C.
- from home to school or to work

2. Point out the parts of the human face:

eyes	forehead	nose	lips
eyebrows	ears	nostrils	chin
eyelashes	ear lobes	cheeks	

Then ask students these questions:

- Where are Roosevelt's glasses?
- Where is Roosevelt's mustache?
- Where is Lincoln's beard?
- Where are your eyebrows?
- Where are your eyelashes?
- Where are your cheeks?
- How do you hear?
- What can you do with your nose?
- What are the two sections of the nose called?

READING COMPREHENSION

A. Mark each of these statements _True_ or _False_.

_____ **1.** The Mount Rushmore heads were carved into black mountains.

_____ **2.** Borglum wanted to carve the regional heroes that Robinson suggested.

_____ **3.** Crazy Horse's carved head will be the same height as Lincoln's.

_____ **4.** Ziolkowski worked on Mount Rushmore and on Thunderhead Mountain.

_____ **5.** The Mount Rushmore heads will look the same a million years from now.

B. Answer these questions about the reading in complete sentences.

1. Why did Robinson want rock carvings in South Dakota?

_____

2. Why did the miners use dynamite on Mount Rushmore?

_____

C. Answer these questions by giving your opinion.

1. Should there be a statue honoring a Sioux in South Dakota? Tell why or why not.

_____

2. Is it a waste of time to carve a statue into a mountain? Tell why or why not.

_____

_____

D. Put a check (✓) in each box if the numbered information is true about that site.

	Mount Rushmore	Crazy Horse
1. completed by the original sculptor		
2. paid for mostly by the government		
3. made of granite		
4. located in South Dakota		
5. a source of Native American pride		
6. still under construction		

VOCABULARY PRACTICE

Say these words aloud, and discuss their meanings. Then use some of them to complete the sentences that follow.

carve	emerge	geologist	regional
crack	figure	granite	repairs
damage	finance	incredible	reservation
drill	forever	models	sculptor
dynamite	funds	plains	treaty

1. _____ is a very hard rock.

2. In 1876, the Sioux had to move to a _____.

3. In South Dakota, the flat areas of land are the _____.

4. The _____ of Crazy Horse will probably _____ from Thunderhead Mountain in the 21st century.

5. A _____ is a formal agreement between two nations.

6. Workers used _____ to remove large amounts of unwanted rock from Mount Rushmore.

7. Something surprising and difficult to believe is _____.

8. Granite sculptures will last a long time, but they won't last _____.

9. A sculptor can _____ figures out of stone or clay.

10. The Mount Rushmore workers made 60-foot heads that looked like the sculptor's _____.

11. Any _____ to the heads (for example, to the _____ across Lincoln's nose) are made by workers.

12. Mount Rushmore is not just a source of _____ pride. It is a national treasure.

ATTRACTIONS *Teacher's Guide*
© 1994 Contemporary Books
A Reproducible Exercise Page

HOMONYMS, SYNONYMS, AND SIMILAR WORDS

Say these pairs of homonyms aloud. Then circle the word that best completes each sentence that follows.

feat / feet   war / wore

1. Carving the Mount Rushmore heads was a difficult (feat, feet).

2. His dancing is terrible! He dances as if he had two left (feat, feet).

3. The soldiers (war, wore) uniforms when they fought in the (war, wore).

PARTS OF SPEECH AND INFLECTED FORMS

Complete these sentences with the correct noun form of the underlined verb. Use this reading or a dictionary for help. Note: Sometimes the verb and the noun are the same.

1. She sculpted a cat from a bar of soap. She made a soap _____.

2. He carved a dog out of a piece of wood. It was a beautiful wood

    _____.

3. When he damaged my car in the accident, he did a lot of _____ to it.

4. The auto mechanic repaired the car. The _____ were very expensive.

5. The government funded the project. The _____ for the project came from the government.

6. When I dropped the dish, it cracked. Now there is a big _____ in it.

7. When he drilled holes in the rock, he used a _____.

8. When you face the sun, you may get a sunburn on your _____.

9. Borglum carved another mountain before he worked on Mount Rushmore. He was an experienced mountain _____.

10. Crazy Horse led his followers in battle. He was a great military _____. His great _____ has not been forgotten.

WORD PARTS

Study the meanings of these word parts from the reading. Then use some of them to complete the words in the sentences that follow.

bi-, bin- = two, both, double; on both sides   *pneum-* = breath, air, gases
fore- = before, the front part of   *re-* = again, back
im-, in-, un- = not   *vis-* = see

1. These drills use compressed air. They are called _____atic drills.

2. If you want to get a closer look at that bird, hold these _____oculars in front of your eyes.

3. That mountain climber's story was very hard to believe. It was an ___credible story.

4. Your _____head is the front part of your head.

5. If you can't be trusted, you're _____trustworthy.

6. A person who can see well has good _____ion.

7. A person who can make intelligent guesses about future conditions has _____sight.

8. I didn't understand the directions. Please ___peat them.

PHRASAL VERBS AND OTHER IDIOMS

Reread the paragraphs in which these idioms are used. The paragraph numbers are given in parentheses. Then write sentences using these idioms.

stand for (3)   run out of (9)   take over (9)
get rid of (7)   off and on (9)   hold up (11)

_____

_____

_____

_____

_____

_____

ATTRACTIONS *Teacher's Guide*
© 1994 Contemporary Books
A Reproducible Exercise Page

PATTERN PRACTICE

A. Prepositional phrases are often used after the verb *to be* in order to tell location. Complete the prepositional phrases in these sentences with one of the words or phrases from the list. You may use a word or phrase more than once.

above	in back of	inside
below	in front of	on
between		

1. Roosevelt's glasses are _____ his nose.

2. Roosevelt's mustache is _____ his lips.

3. Lincoln's beard is _____ his chin.

4. Washington's eyes are _____ his eyebrows.

5. Jefferson's nose is _____ his cheeks.

6. My eyelashes are _____ my eyes.

7. My forehead is _____ my nose.

8. The human brain is _____ the head.

B. Complete these sentences with an appropriate preposition of time. Use *by, in, during, from, on, since,* and *until*.

1. The four presidents on Mount Rushmore represent the nation's greatest accomplishments _____ its first 150 years.

2. Borglum worked on Mount Rushmore _____ 1927 _____ his death _____ 1941.

3. _____ 1941, no further carving has been done on Mount Rushmore.

4. _____ the summer months, Borglum's studio is open to the public.

5. Crazy Horse was killed _____ September 6, 1877.

6. Crazy Horse's sculpted head may emerge from the mountain _____ the year 2000.

ATTRACTIONS *Teacher's Guide*
© 1994 Contemporary Books
A Reproducible Exercise Page

IT'S COLOSSAL: HEADS OF STATE   **31**

PHONICS AND PRONUNCIATION

A. Write in the correct letter(s), *f* or *p*, to complete each phrase. Then read them aloud.

1. a mountain ____eak

2. a ____amous ____resident

3. ____our ____owerful ____ighters

4. ____ederal ____unding

5. a ____riendly ____erson

6. a ____ive-____oot ____laster model

7. ____oreign ____olicy

8. ____inished ____rojects

B. The sound *z* is made by the letter *z* and often by the letter *s*. Read the sentences below aloud. Then circle all the letters that spell the *z* sound.

1. Please close the screen door before the bugs fly in.

2. Stay close to your sister so you don't get lost.

3. Hang your clothes in the hall closet.

4. If you close the windows, it may get very close [warm and uncomfortable] in here.

5. The repairs on the car were very expensive.

C. Read these pairs of words aloud. Circle the letters that spell the *z* sound. Underline the letters that spell the *s* sound.

his / history   advice / advise   please / police
sure / surface   truck / truce   recent / result
press / president   crazy / crass   zoo / sue

ATTRACTIONS *Teacher's Guide*
© 1994 Contemporary Books
A Reproducible Exercise Page

HISTORY IN STONE

(PAGES 57–67)

Pre-Reading Activities

Discussion Questions

1. About the Grand Canyon: Have you ever seen the Grand Canyon? Can you describe it? Where did you stand? What was the view? Have you seen a picture of the Grand Canyon?

2. About the notion of the Grand Canyon as a barrier: What is a barrier? What other physical barriers have you seen in nature? Rivers? Mountains? Lakes? What are other types of physical barriers? (detours, one-way signs, etc.) Can you think of other uses of the word *barrier*? (*language barrier, sound barrier*, etc.)

3. About the notion of "history in stone": How can we learn about a place from reading what nature has left behind? Can we also learn the history of a place from what people have left behind? The Indians, for example, left sites where pottery, weapons, and farming tools were found. Do we leave a history when we move out of a house or an apartment? What history have you left behind in a former residence?

4. About national parks: (Explain to students that the United States has 50 national parks under the jurisdiction of the federal government. Yellowstone is the oldest, founded in 1892.) Is this a good way for government to protect land? Do tourists harm these beautiful places in any way? Do tourists improve them in some ways?

5. About the teaser: What is the difference in distance "as the crow flies" versus by road? What is the difference in traveling the same trip by foot or by car? (22 miles versus 215.) (Natural barriers such as mountains or bodies of water can make getting from one point to another longer.)

Section Headings

"A Master Stonecutter": Make certain that everyone understands the metaphor of the river as craftsperson fashioning the Grand Canyon through the process of erosion.

Important Vocabulary from the Reading

1. Have students scan the reading for words about nature such as *barrier, erosion, fossils, waterfalls, rapids, desert, petrified wood, crystals*. Discuss the meaning of these words. Then have students brainstorm and try to think of other words about nature. You may want to have them do this in groups, giving each group a different setting: forest, mountains, beach, etc.

2. Words pertaining to history that you might discuss with the class are *civilization, missionary, treaty*, and *territory*.

Activities to Accompany the Reading

Playing Word Games

Point out the root *-gamy*, which means "marriage." Have students define the terms *polygamy, monogamy*, and *bigamy*.

Improvising Scenes

1. Have a student pretend he is John Wesley Powell convincing other people to join his expedition.

2. Have a group of students pretend that they are visiting the Grand Canyon. Have them debate about what they would like to see there.

Summarizing Chronology

After they have read the section headed "Star 48," have students summarize the history of Arizona before it became a state. Have them draw a time line based on the information provided.

Using Maps

On a map of the United States, have students locate Arizona. Have them find Mexico, New Mexico, Utah, Colorado, and Wyoming, all mentioned in the reading. Have them find the Four Corners Monument and trace the path of the Colorado River.

Studying Word Parts to Build Vocabulary

Point out the negative prefix *un-*, meaning "not," as in *unpopular*. Have them discuss other *un-* phrases from the reading such as *uninhabited Indian sites* and *unusual petrified trees*.

Reading for Details

Have students read the Sidelights section. Ask them how many foreign tourists visit the Grand Canyon each year. Ask them how many people live in Arizona.

Discussion, Writing, or Research Topics

Have students select one of the following topics, do library research on it, and then work with classmates to prepare a group presentation for the class:

- the Havasupai Indians
- the Anasazi Indians
- the Hopi Indians
- Francisco Vásquez de Coronado
- Major John Wesley Powell
- President Theodore Roosevelt and national parks
- the 1877 silver rush at Tombstone, Arizona
- fossilization
- erosion

Extension Activities

1. Much Western history took place in Arizona. Have the class watch movies about Kit Carson, Arizona Indian scout; Wyatt Earp, once the deputy sheriff of Tombstone; and Geronimo. Also, the 1990s movies *Thelma and Louise*, *Grand Canyon*, *Tombstone*, and *Geronimo* have important scenes in or near Arizona.

2. Take students on a field trip to a local museum where fossils, dinosaur skeletons, and possibly petrified wood are displayed. Many museums also have fine Native American exhibits.

For ESL Students

1. Ask ESL students if any natural wonders exist in their native countries (mountains, waterfalls, volcanoes, etc.). Ask them to bring pictures, if available.

2. On the chalkboard, provide students with the conversion information below. Write the four sentences that follow on the board, and then have them fill in the correct information. For help, have students reread the paragraphs indicated.

   449 kilometers = approximately 279 miles
   21 kilometers = approximately 13 miles
   1,609 meters = approximately 1 mile
   23 centimeters = approximately 9 inches

   - The Grand Canyon is _____ meters deep. (1)
   - It is _____ miles long. (1)
   - At its widest, it is _____ kilometers wide. (1)
   - Average rainfall is _____ centimeters a year. (17)

   Then have students convert these measurements back to miles, kilometers, or inches.

3. Have students write sentences using these measurement words: *kilometers*, *meters*, *centimeters*, *miles*, and *inches*.

READING COMPREHENSION

A. Mark each of these statements *True* or *False*.

_____ **1.** The Rio Grande created the Grand Canyon.

_____ **2.** Four million tourists a day visit the Grand Canyon.

_____ **3.** John Wesley Powell visited the Grand Canyon only once.

_____ **4.** Three million people once lived in the immediate area of the Grand Canyon.

_____ **5.** If you are under 4 feet 7 inches, you can't ride a mule to Phantom Ranch.

_____ **6.** Arizona was once owned by France.

_____ **7.** Jefferson Davis was the first governor of Arizona.

B. What does each word mean in the paragraph indicated? Circle the letter of the correct answer.

1. barrier (1): (a) fence (b) something that prevents passage

2. gathered (4): (a) collected (b) understood

3. remote (8): (a) faraway (b) device for controlling a TV

4. admission (10): (a) entrance (b) confession

5. stormy (21): (a) characterized by violent changes (b) windy and rainy

6. supported (24): (a) paid for (b) favored

7. bill (24): (a) a draft of a law (b) a fee charged for services

VOCABULARY PRACTICE

A. Use some of these words to complete the sentences that follow.

ancient   permission   superstition
helicopter   plunged   tended
isolated   reshapes

1. To ski the North Rim in winter, you need special _____.

2. Mormon settlers _____ their sheep on the rocky land.

3. The Mormons lived in a very _____ place.

4. Erosion changes the climate and the geography. It _____ the land over time.

5. There was a _____ that stealing the petrified wood caused bad luck.

B. Use some of these compound words to complete the sentences that follow.

backpack   nowhere   underwater
businessman   overnight   wildflowers
firewood   sunset

1. At the North Rim, there are many beautiful _____.

2. Ancient _____ animals can now be seen as fossils in the walls of the Grand Canyon.

3. You can stay _____ at Phantom Ranch.

4. A mule can carry your _____ for an extra $60!

5. The first governor of Arizona was a _____.

ATTRACTIONS *Teacher's Guide*
© 1994 Contemporary Books
A Reproducible Exercise Page

HOMONYMS, SYNONYMS, AND SIMILAR WORDS

These word pairs are homonyms. (They sound the same.)

site / sight   great / grate   deer / dear

Say the homonyms above aloud, and then use them to complete these sentences.

1. The Grand Canyon is a _____ natural wonder.

2. The Anasazi hunted _____.

3. The bride and groom were a beautiful _____ to see.

4. Every year, a few people lose their lives at this famous _____.

5. Many national parks are _____ to the hearts of Americans, so they are visited frequently.

6. In the city, your keys can fall down a _____. At the Grand Canyon, they can fall off a cliff!

PARTS OF SPEECH AND INFLECTED FORMS

Complete these sentences with the correct verb form of the underlined word.

1. Nature did the <u>carving</u>. Nature _____ the Grand Canyon.

2. The Indians went <u>hunting</u> with spears. They _____ in order to eat.

3. In pioneer times, <u>trapping</u> animals was common. People _____ animals for fur and food.

4. <u>Visiting</u> the North Rim is difficult in winter. She couldn't _____ the North Rim in February.

5. <u>Exploring</u> the canyon on foot can be dangerous. He took a first aid kit along when he _____ the canyon.

WORD PARTS

Study the meanings of these words from the reading. Then use some of them to complete the sentences that follow.

discovered   included   reshapes
embedded   preserved   returned
extended   removes   unemployed

1. In 1975, the borders of the park were _____. The park doubled in size.

2. Fossils are _____ animals and plants.

3. John Wesley Powell _____ for a second tour of the Grand Canyon.

4. Gold was never _____ by Coronado and his men.

5. Crystals were _____ in the petrified wood.

6. The first governor of Arizona came to the state as an _____ miner.

PHRASAL VERBS AND OTHER IDIOMS

Reread the paragraphs that the idioms in the column on the left are used in. Then match each idiom with its definition in the column on the right. Write the correct letters on the blank lines.

_____ **1.** lose your footing (3)   **(a)** indicates the location

_____ **2.** come in search of (6)   **(b)** ride a horse

_____ **3.** run the rapids (7)   **(c)** seek

_____ **4.** stay in the saddle (14)   **(d)** steer a boat through
                                                            fast-moving water

_____ **5.** be in good health (14)   **(e)** trip or fall

_____ **6.** marks the spot (20)   **(f)** not be ill

ATTRACTIONS *Teacher's Guide*
© 1994 Contemporary Books
A Reproducible Exercise Page

PATTERN PRACTICE

A. Complete these statements using words with the appropriate *-er* or *-est* ending.

1. The Grand Canyon is _____ than it is wide.

2. Yellowstone National Park was the first to be dedicated. It is _____ than Grand Canyon National Park.

3. The Grand Canyon is one of the world's _____ barriers.

4. Arizona has a _____ number of Native Americans than most other states.

5. Retired people like a warm, dry climate _____ than a cold, wet one.

B. Use the *-er* and *-est* words above in your own sentences.

1. _____

2. _____

3. _____

4. _____

5. _____

C. Write questions about some of the people discussed in this reading. Begin each question with *Who was* or *Who were*. Then answer your questions.

Example: Who was John Wesley Powell?
He was an early explorer of the Grand Canyon.

1. Question: _____

   Answer: _____

2. Question: _____

   Answer: _____

PHONICS AND PRONUNCIATION

A. Say the following pairs of words aloud.

canyon / cannon   carving / craving
wild / wilderness   wood / food
booths / tooth   collection / correction

Use eight of the words above in sentences of your own. Use a dictionary if you are unsure of the meanings.

_____

_____

_____

_____

_____

_____

_____

_____

B. Answer the following questions using past-tense verbs, and then read your answers aloud. Be sure to pronounce the -ed endings correctly. There are three pronunciations: t, d, and id.

1. How many tourists visited the Grand Canyon last year?

_____

2. Were Spanish explorers interested in fossils?

_____

3. What is displayed at the Conscience Wood exhibit?

_____

4. Can you have your car checked at the Desert View Watchtower?

_____

ATTRACTIONS *Teacher's Guide*
© 1994 Contemporary Books
A Reproducible Exercise Page

DISNEY'S WORLD

(PAGES 71–81)

Pre-Reading Activities

Discussion Questions

1. About amusement parks and theme parks: What's the difference between an ordinary amusement park and a theme park? What theme parks have you visited?

2. About Walt Disney cartoon characters: Can you describe some Walt Disney cartoon characters? Are they like real animals?

3. About space travel: Would you like to travel to another planet? Why? Where? Have you ever watched the launching of a spaceship? Describe what you saw and heard.

4. About the teaser: How big is Walt Disney World? (The area of Walt Disney World, not just the three parks but the entire resort, is about twice the size of Manhattan. The answer is found in paragraph 3. Students may be surprised that Walt Disney World is so big and that Manhattan is so small.)

Section Headings

"Happiness for Sale": Ask students how this heading differs from the subheads in this chapter. Ask students what is covered under this heading. (Disney World)

"Beyond Walt Disney World": Ask students what is covered under this heading. (This section discusses the other tourist sites in central Florida.)

"Blast Off!": Ask students if this is a heading or a subhead.

Important Vocabulary from the Reading

1. Compare and contrast the words *amusement, pleasure,* and *entertainment.*

2. Discuss these words commonly used at Disney parks: *monorail, pavilion, production, Audio-Animatronics, mosaic, animation, cartoon,* and *production.*

3. Discuss this vocabulary associated with space flight: *launch, satellite, orbit, astronaut, lunar, module, space station.*

4. Discuss various meanings of the word *theme.*

5. Discuss the meaning of *simulated* and *simulation.*

6. Discuss the relationship between the word *refuge* (used in the phrase *wildlife refuge* in this chapter) and the word *refugee.*

Activities to Accompany the Reading

Playing Word Games

1. Have students list in three minutes all the words they can that relate to outer space. Then put the lists on the blackboard and ask for definitions.

2. Explain to students that the name EPCOT is an acronym, a word formed from the letters or syllables in a name or phrase. Have students work in small groups to see how many other acronyms they can think of. Another acronym from this chapter is *laser.* Another common one is *radar.* Have each group put its list on the board, and determine the winner. Then have each group tell the term each acronym represents.

Improvising Scenes

1. Have students role-play three tourists on their way to Walt Disney World arguing about which park to go to first.

2. Have students role-play a group of astronauts traveling in space discussing the view from the window.

Comparing and Contrasting

Compare and contrast California and Florida. Compare and contrast Disneyland and Walt Disney World. Tell students that the Magic Kingdom of Walt Disney World was modeled after Disneyland. But, in recent years, Disneyland has been expanded. It now includes a theme park devoted to movies and cartoons.

Using Maps

1. Have students locate Anaheim, California, and Orlando, Florida, on a map of the United States. Ask them to guess about how many miles apart they are. (It's roughly 3,000 miles from the Atlantic Coast to the Pacific Coast.)

2. Have students find Cape Canaveral on a map.

3. Locate some other important cities and tourist spots in Florida. Point out St. Augustine, which is the oldest American city settled by Europeans.

Discussion, Writing, or Research Topics

Have students reread paragraphs 4–6. Then discuss with the class the Disney quotation "We are selling happiness." Ask students to list some of the characteristics of Disney parks that make people happy. Have students discuss them and/or write about them. Students may point out that the parks provide excitement, surprise, beauty, a clean environment, and cheerful employees. They are places where families can have a good time together, and they appeal to all age groups. Students may think the sights are so overwhelming that they can make almost anyone forget his or her problems. Ask students if there is something wrong with the idea of selling happiness because happiness is something that people must create for themselves. Students might argue that no commercial environment can bring a person lasting happiness.

Extension Activities

1. Students may enjoy reading a biography of Walt Disney. It is an amazing "rags to riches" story. One book-length biography that is simply written is Katherine Barrett and Richard Greene's *The Man Behind the Magic: The Story of Walt Disney*, published in New York by Viking Penguin in 1991.

2. Show the class some Disney films and videos, such as the following:

   - short videos about the parks, which sell for about $19.95 and are available from Walt Disney Attractions, Incorporated, Lake Buena Vista, FL 32830 or at a Disney store
   - Disney cartoons featuring Mickey Mouse or Donald Duck
   - *Fantasia*, a classic film in which Disney animation is set to classical music

For ESL Students

1. To develop listening skills, read the class the following story about how the city of Orlando got its name: This story happened in central Florida in the 1840s. A group of American soldiers were exploring a dangerous wilderness. The American government had asked all Native Americans to leave the area. But some were still in Florida, hiding from the soldiers. One evening, a group of soldiers camped outdoors for the night. All of them went to sleep except Orlando Reeves. He had to stay awake because he was on guard duty. In the darkness, Reeves heard a noise. He wondered, was there someone out there, or was it just a rolling log? Suddenly, Reeves knew the answer. It was an Indian attacker disguised with branches from trees. Reeves fired his gun to warn the other soldiers. They woke up. Reeves saved their lives, but he couldn't save his own. The Indian's arrow killed him. To honor this brave soldier, in 1857, the place got a new name—Orlando.

   Have students retell the story in their own words, or ask them questions about it.

2. Tell the story of Cinderella with help from students who know it. Ask students whether the story is any different in other countries.

3. Ask students the following questions: What does "It's a small world" mean? Is the world getting smaller? In what sense?

READING COMPREHENSION

A. Mark each of these statements *True* or *False*.

_____ **1.** The ride "It's a Small World" is in the World Showcase section of EPCOT Center.

_____ **2.** In Walt Disney World's Cinderella Castle, the story of Cinderella is told in pictures made from pieces of stone and colored glass.

_____ **3.** Some Audio-Animatronic figures walk and talk.

_____ **4.** On a simulated ride, passengers travel in moving vehicles that run on railroad tracks.

_____ **5.** Disney-MGM Studios is both a theme park and a real movie and TV production studio.

B. On the blank line, write the letter of the word that best completes each comparison.

1. north:south

as west:____ (a) west coast (b) northwest (c) east (d) direction

2. Disneyland:Anaheim

as Walt Disney World:____ (a) Florida (b) Orlando (c) Paris (d) theme park

3. sailor:boat

as astronaut:____ (a) airplane (b) space suit (c) spaceship (d) rocket

4. Future World:EPCOT

as Kennedy Space Center:____ (a) astronauts (b) Orlando (c) Walt Disney World (d) Cape Canaveral

5. boat:moving vehicle

as Mickey Mouse:____ (a) cartoon character (b) Minnie Mouse (c) Walt Disney (d) animated film

VOCABULARY PRACTICE

A. Write one of these verbs on each blank line to make a phrase. (Some verbs make sense with more than one of the nouns that follow.)

avoid	fire	orbit
board	hum	risk
combine	obtain	share

1. _____ trouble

2. _____ a melody

3. _____ injury

4. _____ a train

5. _____ a rocket

6. _____ the Earth

7. _____ rides and shows

8. _____ expenses

B. Circle the word or words that don't belong in each group.

1. a theme park: Magic Kingdom, Orlando, Sea World, EPCOT

2. a body of water: lagoon, pond, lake, tunnel, river

3. a country in World Showcase: Canada, France, Germany, India, Italy

4. a moving vehicle: stroller, pavilion, wheelchair, gondola, spaceship

5. a method of communication: radio, television, film, audiotape, prototype

C. Match each word in the column on the left with its opposite in the column on the right. Write the correct letters on the blank lines.

_____ **1.** elevated

_____ **2.** emotional

_____ **3.** familiar

_____ **4.** genuine

_____ **5.** permanent

(a) temporary

(b) rational

(c) unusual

(d) simulated

(e) underground

ATTRACTIONS *Teacher's Guide*
© 1994 Contemporary Books
A Reproducible Exercise Page

HOMONYMS, SYNONYMS, AND SIMILAR WORDS

Circle the word that best completes each sentence.

1. The words of that song have an important (message, massage).

2. Kennedy Space Center is the main (lunch, launch) site for the United States space program.

3. EPCOT (obtains, contains) two main sections—Future World and World Showcase.

4. A (satellite, stalemate) circles the Earth.

5. A building with a ramp is (access, accessible) to people in wheelchairs.

6. If you get a lot for the money you spend, you have gotten a (bargain, barroom).

7. People enjoy walking through a (hunted, haunted) house if the ghosts and skeletons aren't real.

8. We didn't really travel anywhere. But we felt like we were flying through outer space. It was a (simulated, stimulated) ride.

9. A wildlife (refuge, refugee) is a safe place for animals.

10. People go to Pleasure Island to enjoy the (nightlife, wildlife) there.

PARTS OF SPEECH AND INFLECTED FORMS

A. Write the noun form of each adjective. Use a dictionary for help, if necessary.

1. accessible _____

2. adventurous _____

3. amusing _____

4. dangerous _____

5. happy _____

6. imaginary _____

7. nutritious _____

8. pleasant _____

9. risky _____

10. symbolic _____

B. How many common noun endings can you find in the words you wrote above? _____ Write them on the line.

_____

WORD PARTS

Study the meanings of these word parts. Then use some of them to complete the words in the sentences that follow.

aero- = air, aircraft	*audio-* = hearing	*proto-* = first, original
anima- = life, breath	*mono-* = one, alone, single	*techno-* = art, skill
astro- = star		

1. _____tion is a method of making drawings look alive on screen.

2. A person who travels in space is called an _____naut.

3. An original design or model is called a _____type.

4. An _____meter is a machine for testing a person's hearing.

5. The _____logy of Disney's Audio-Animatronic figures is amazing.

6. This elevated train runs on one track, so it's called a _____rail.

PHRASAL VERBS AND OTHER IDIOMS

Reread the paragraphs that these idioms are used in. The paragraph numbers are in parentheses. Then use some of the idioms to complete the sentences that follow.

run-down (2)	stands for (16)	blast off (above 22)
year-round (3)	sound effects (17)	running start (22)
feel sour (4)	spend a fortune (19)	headed for (23)

1. The owner doesn't take care of that building. He doesn't fix things when they break. The building is _____.

2. The term EPCOT is an acronym. It _____ Experimental Prototype Community of Tomorrow.

3. In movies and on TV, noises such as footsteps, doorbells, and gunshots are _____.

4. We're driving east from Walt Disney World. We're _____ Cape Canaveral.

5. Walt Disney World is open _____.

ATTRACTIONS *Teacher's Guide*
© 1994 Contemporary Books
A Reproducible Exercise Page

PATTERN PRACTICE

A. Reread paragraph 19. Then give some advice to a friend who's going to Walt Disney World.

Example: You'd better <u>make a motel reservation before you go.</u>

1. You should _____ .

2. You ought to _____ .

3. You'd better _____ .

4. You shouldn't _____ .

5. You'd better not _____ .

6. You can _____ .

7. You can't _____ .

B. Use information from the reading to complete the adjective clauses in these sentences.

Example: Florida, <u>which is a southern state</u>, has a mild climate.

1. Walt Disney, who _____ , had the idea to build theme parks.

2. Walt Disney World, which _____ , is the largest theme park in the world.

3. The Kennedy Space Center is on Cape Canaveral, Florida, which

   _____ .

4. Cinderella Castle, which _____ , is beautiful.

5. Walt Disney, whose _____ , was a very creative person.

PHONICS AND PRONUNCIATION

A. Complete these words using the correct vowels. These words are all pronounced with two vowel sounds in a row. Read the words aloud.

aud____   aquar____m   med____val   mos____c

B. Read these words spelled with *ou* aloud.

ow: sound, thousand, sour   *uh*: country
aw: bought   *oo*: tourist, through, souvenir

Write the correct pronunciation for the underlined letters.

th<u>ou</u>ght: [   ]   c<u>ou</u>sin: [   ]   c<u>ou</u>rt: [   ]   f<u>ou</u>ntain: [   ]

C. Say these words spelled with *au*. The vowel sound is the same as in *tall*.

audio   astronaut   launch   haunted

Write two more words in which the letters *au* are pronounced as the *a* in *tall*.

_____   _____

D. Say these words containing the long *u* sound. It's pronounced as in the word *you*. Circle the letters that spell the long *u* sound.

beautiful   educational   huge   universal
computer   future   module   usual

E. Read these sentences aloud. Circle the letters that spell the short *u* sound (*u* as in *cup*).

1. Did the astronauts have lunch before the launch?

2. We went through the haunted house at Magic Kingdom.

3. They hunted huge wild animals in the jungle.

4. The tourists bought some beautiful souvenirs.

5. We ate hot and sour soup at a Chinese restaurant.

ATTRACTIONS *Teacher's Guide*
© 1994 Contemporary Books
A Reproducible Exercise Page

A LIVING MUSEUM
(PAGES 3–13)

Pre-Reading Activities
Discussion Questions

1. About the Pilgrims: What do you know about the Pilgrims? What would you like to find out about the Pilgrims by reading the selection?

2. About the Pilgrims' journey: When did they come to America? How many were on the ship? What was the ship's name? Where did it land?

3. About the first Thanksgiving: In what year did it take place? Do historians know the exact date? What did the Pilgrims eat? Who were their guests? How long did the celebration last?

4. About the Thanksgiving holiday today: When is it? What are the major customs?

5. About the teaser: Did the Pilgrims really land on Plymouth Rock? (Descendants of *Mayflower* passengers say that, according to their ancestors, the Pilgrims really did land next to Plymouth Rock. See paragraph 3.)

Section Headings

"Time Travel Made Easy": The six headings in this reading are quite literal descriptions of the section contents, except for the first one. Ask students why the authors began with a reference to time travel. That is really the purpose of Plimoth Plantation. It is a stimulus to the imagination. Its first-person historical accounts are designed to enhance the feeling of really being in Plymouth in 1627.

Important Vocabulary from the Reading

1. Make sure that students understand the usual meaning of the words *pilgrim* and *pilgrimage* so that they realize why Bradford called the Separatists Pilgrims.

2. Discuss the meanings of the following terms from the text: *costumed guides, intended landing place, military drills, overeager tourists,* and *shearing sheep.*

3. Discuss the meanings of *hammock, venture,* and *wampum.*

Activities to Accompany the Reading
Playing Word Games

1. In this game, students sit in circles of about six people. The first person begins with a statement such as "I visited Plimoth Plantation, and I saw a turkey" (or a Pilgrim, Priscilla Mullins, chickens, etc.). Each person repeats all the items said before and adds one of his or her own. Each item named must be something that would actually be in Plimoth. If a player omits one of the items, he or she is "out." The winners are the last players remaining in each circle.

2. List these words on the chalkboard. In this game, students search in the paragraphs indicated for the antonyms of the words listed. This game can be played with partners and a time limit.

temporary (2)   plentiful (14)
sinking (3)   many (26)
freed (7)   friends (26)
safe (8)   die (27)
weak (11)   mourn (28)

Improvising Scenes

1. Have students improvise the following scenes from "The Courtship of Miles Standish":

- Miles asks John to propose to Priscilla for him.
- John asks Priscilla to marry Miles, and she responds.

2. Have students improvise Samoset's arrival at Plymouth Colony. Remind them that his English was limited.

Summarizing

Have students write a summary of one of the following:

- the *Mayflower*'s voyage across the Atlantic Ocean
- the sights that a visitor sees at Plimoth Plantation

Using Maps

1. On a map of the United States, find Cape Cod. Provincetown, where the *Mayflower* landed, is on the tip of Cape Cod. The ship stayed in Provincetown Harbor. After the men discovered the cleared area at Plymouth, the ship went across Cape Cod Bay to Plymouth Harbor. Point this trip out on the map.

2. Find Jamestown, Virginia, where the first permanent English colony in America was established in 1607. Discuss why the Pilgrims might have preferred the climate there.

Discussion, Writing, or Research Topics

1. Discuss with the class or have students write about the purpose of places that re-create the past or about what visitors gain by looking backward.

2. Discuss with the class or have students write about what the Pilgrims would find strange if they traveled forward in time to the present century.

3. Students might want to read more about 17th-century colonial life in America. Then they might choose an aspect of colonial life to take notes about: food, marriage, family life, occupational training, education, architecture, or religious beliefs. Have students present a panel discussion on each topic. Students might also research the mysterious disappearance and reappearance of Bradford's history of the Pilgrims.

Extension Activities

1. Have students read some sections of "The Courtship of Miles Standish" aloud in class. Tell the conclusion of the story: John proposes to Priscilla only after he hears that Miles has been killed. After the wedding ceremony, Miles walks in and begs their forgiveness.

2. Have students research Williamsburg, Virginia. It is another historic city that has been preserved and restored. Tourists see it as it looked in the 18th century.

3. Have six students debate the following issue: Today's American immigrants have a more difficult time than the Pilgrims did. Have three students debate for the resolution and three against. Have the class cast ballots to determine the winning team.

For ESL Students

1. Discuss these aspects of the modern American Thanksgiving:

   - the date
   - the traditional foods
   - the holiday as a time for family reunions

2. Introduce Thanksgiving recipes. Reading recipes is a good way to teach nonmetric measurements and abbreviations. Bring a set of measuring cups and measuring spoons to class to show. Bring recipes of some traditional Thanksgiving foods that students might want to make at home: turkey, stuffing, cranberries, sweet potatoes, squash, pumpkin pie.

3. Share a Thanksgiving meal. If students are interested, plan a class meal including traditional Thanksgiving foods. This might include cold, sliced turkey sandwiches with cranberry sauce and pumpkin pie. An alternative would be to have a class Thanksgiving meal together in the school cafeteria or a nearby restaurant.

4. Show a videotape about the Pilgrims. A series called *The Shaping of the American Nation* includes two titles: "The Puritan Experience: Forsaking England" and "The Puritan Experience: Making a New World." These were produced by Learning Corporation of America at 1350 Avenue of the Americas, New York, NY 10019, (212) 397-9360.

READING COMPREHENSION

A. Mark each of these statements *True* or *False*.

_____ **1.** There were a total of 127 people on the *Mayflower*.

_____ **2.** Only the Separatists signed the Mayflower Compact.

_____ **3.** The original *Mayflower* crossed the Atlantic Ocean faster than *Mayflower II*.

_____ **4.** Columbus's ships crossed the Atlantic faster than the *Mayflower* did.

_____ **5.** Plimoth Plantation is a copy of Plymouth Colony as it looked in 1621.

_____ **6.** The Plymouth colonists spoke several different languages.

B. Make inferences (based on the information in the paragraphs indicated) to complete these sentences.

1. The Puritans who left the Church of England were called Separatists because (6)

_____.

2. The Pilgrims didn't light a fire on the ship when it was windy because (11)

_____.

3. The baby that was born on the *Mayflower* was named Oceanus because (11)

_____.

4. Henry Hornblower II built Plimoth Plantation because (1, 2, 17)

_____.

5. During meals, the Pilgrims used large napkins because (30)

_____.

6. The Pilgrims found a cleared site to build their village on because

_____. (Sidelights)

VOCABULARY PRACTICE

A. Say these words aloud. Then use some of them to complete the sentences that follow.

beverages	complained	introduced
colony	established	profits
community	harvest	recruited

1. English businessmen _____ people to travel to America because they could profit from the venture.

2. The Pilgrims _____ Plymouth Colony in 1620.

3. In Plymouth Colony, water and beer were the most common _____, even for children.

4. The Indians helped the Pilgrims plant crops in the spring, and the colonists had a good _____ that fall.

5. The Indians also _____ the Pilgrims to new foods.

6. For several years, the colonists shared their _____ with the businessmen who financed their voyage.

B. Match each word in the column on the left with the correct phrase in the column on the right. Write the correct letters on the blank lines.

_____ 1. governor

_____ 2. orphan

_____ 3. passenger

_____ 4. teenager

_____ 5. widower

(a) the leader of a colony or state

(b) a man whose wife is dead

(c) a child whose parents are dead

(d) someone riding on or in a moving vehicle

(e) someone aged 13–19

ATTRACTIONS *Teacher's Guide*
© 1994 Contemporary Books
A Reproducible Exercise Page

HOMONYMS, SYNONYMS, AND SIMILAR WORDS

A. Complete these sentences using the homonyms *piece* and *peace*.

1. The quiet of the woods and the beautiful scenery gave me a sense of _____.

2. That _____ of cake was larger than I had expected.

Read these sentences containing the word *tip*:

Give that nice waiter a big <u>tip</u>.

The cup <u>tipped</u> over, and the coffee spilled out.

The Pilgrims landed on the <u>tip</u> of Cape Cod.

Read these sentences containing the word *left*:

How many apples do we have <u>left</u>?

Do you eat with your <u>left</u> hand or your right?

The *Mayflower* <u>left</u> Massachusetts in April of 1621.

B. Now use some of the homonyms and underlined words above to complete this story.

(1) My family ate Thanksgiving dinner in a restaurant last year. (2) When we finished the meal, there was no turkey _____ on the table and no room _____ in our stomachs. (3) The waiter brought some pumpkin pie. We each ate a big _____ of that. (4) As he was pouring the coffee, the waiter _____ over a glass of water into my lap. (5) I didn't care. The meal was so good that we _____ him a big _____ anyway.

BOOK 2

WORD PARTS

A. Study the meanings of these word parts from the reading. Then use them to complete the words that follow.

inter- = between, among	*mal-* = bad	*re-* = again, back
-less = without	*mis-* = wrong	*trans-* = across

1. create again: _____-create

2. carry across: _____port

3. something incorrect: _____take

4. not dangerous: harm_____

5. illness caused by an unhealthy diet: _____nutrition

6. a person who explains, translates, or otherwise aids communication between people: _____preter

B. The reading contains four words that begin with *over-*. Discuss the meanings of *overboard*, *overeager*, *overwork*, and *overexposure*. Write two other compound words that begin with *over*.

_____   _____

C. Write two words that contain the word part *trans-*.

_____   _____

D. Using noun endings *-er*, *-or*, or *-ist*, write the word for a person who does each of these actions.

1. governs _____

2. leads people _____

3. sails a ship _____

4. lives in a colony _____

5. tours a place _____

6. visits a place _____

ATTRACTIONS *Teacher's Guide*
© 1994 Contemporary Books
A Reproducible Exercise Page

PHRASAL VERBS AND OTHER IDIOMS

A. Reread the paragraphs these phrasal verbs are used in. The paragraph numbers are in parentheses. Then use some of the phrasal verbs to complete the sentences that follow.

go on (2)   locked up (7)   made it (12)
turned (someone) in (7)   grew up (7)   cut down (14)

1. The English police _____ the Separatists _____.

2. When the Separatists tried to escape to Holland, the ship's captain _____ them _____.

3. It was a rough journey, but the *Mayflower* _____ _____ across the ocean to America.

4. The men needed logs to build homes. So they _____ _____ some trees.

5. The children who _____ _____ in Plymouth Colony worked hard.

B. Discuss the meanings of these expressions:

agreed to   was/were supposed to
had to   was/were worried about

Now use them to complete these sentences.

1. The *Mayflower* _____ go to Virginia. But it went to Massachusetts instead.

2. The Pilgrims _____ the many dangers in an unsettled land.

3. The men _____ make and obey laws.

4. The Pilgrims _____ live on the ship until the men built homes.

5. Pilgrim children _____ help their parents with the work of the colony.

BOOK 2

PATTERN PRACTICE

A. Complete these sentences by writing an appropriate preposition of time. Use one of these: *about, by, during, in, on, since.*

1. _____ 375 years ago, the Pilgrims came to America.

2. _____ September 6, 1620, the *Mayflower* left England.

3. _____ the time that the Pilgrims were building their homes, many of them lived on the *Mayflower*.

4. _____ April 1621, all of the Pilgrims had homes.

5. _____ the fourth Thursday in November, Americans celebrate Thanksgiving.

6. _____ 1620, descendants of the *Mayflower* passengers have lived in America.

B. Write two sentences that begin with prepositions of time.

1. _____

2. _____

PARTS OF SPEECH AND INFLECTED FORMS

Write a noun form of each verb listed. Use a dictionary for help, if necessary. Note: Sometimes the noun and verb are the same. Also, some verbs have more than one noun.

Examples: introduce <u>introduction</u>   establish <u>establishment</u>

1. attend _____   6. propose _____

2. bury _____   7. settle _____

3. complain _____   8. survive _____

4. harvest _____   9. supply _____

5. profit _____   10. wave _____

ATTRACTIONS *Teacher's Guide*
© 1994 Contemporary Books
A Reproducible Exercise Page

AMERICA'S HOME

(PAGES 17–27)

Pre-Reading Activities

Discussion Questions

1. About the history of the White House: When was it built? Who was the first president to live there?

2. About its location: Where is it? What is its famous address?

3. About its uses: What are some of its uses in addition to being the home of the president?

4. About famous areas: What are some of the famous rooms and gardens?

5. About changes: Over two centuries, what changes have been made? What improvements do you assume have been added?

6. About employees: How many people do you think work there? (See paragraph 24.)

7. About the teaser: The ghost of which U.S. president walks the White House halls? (Lincoln's ghost has been sighted frequently. See paragraph 25.)

Section Headings

"The President's Residence": The heading suggests an introductory section.

"A Quick Tour": The heading indicates that the section tells about the standard tour given to tourists.

"Building the White House": This heading reveals that the section begins a chronological account of the White House from the planning stages.

"Rebuilding and Adding": This heading indicates a continuation of the chronology, telling about further changes made and about the expansion of the building over time.

"A $6 Million Face-Lift": This heading suggests major remodeling.

"The World of the White House": The heading indicates that information about life inside the White House will be presented.

Important Vocabulary from the Reading

1. The White House is called the Executive Mansion. Students should understand that *executive* refers to one of the three branches of the government. This is a good time to review the meaning and responsibilities of each branch—executive, legislative, and judicial.

2. Some homonyms to review:

   • *capital* and *Capitol*: Show a photo of the Capitol to be sure that students do not confuse the Capitol and the White House. Be sure that they understand what each building is used for. Also, discuss the various meanings of the word *capital* (its meaning in business and finance, etc.).

   • *aid* and *aide*: The word *aid* can be used as a verb or a noun. As a noun, it refers to a helpful thing. The word *aide* refers to a person who assists.

3. The words *ghost*, *haunt*, and *transparent* are all in the reading and all relate to ghosts. Discuss the difference between the words *transparent* and *invisible*.

4. Tell students that the White House bicentennial was in 1992. Point out the meanings of the word parts *bi-* and *cent-*. Ask students what other bicentennial celebrations they've heard of (the Declaration of Independence, the U.S. Constitution) and what centennials they may remember from other readings (the Statue of Liberty).

5. Discuss various phrases beginning with *public* and *private*. (The reading has *public housing* and *private contributions*.) Ask what is usually meant when we say something is public. (It suggests that something is available to citizens and supported by tax dollars from a governmental body. *Private* suggests that something is available to certain people only and is not supported by tax dollars.)

6. Discuss some difficult phrases from the reading, such as *crystal chandelier*.

7. Discuss the word *foundation*. In this reading, it refers to the structure that supports a building, but students should know its related meaning, "a charitable organization that supports good work."

Activities to Accompany the Reading

Playing Word Games

Give students ten minutes to scan the reading and write down all the compound words they can find. Determine the winner. Then be sure students know the meanings of all the words listed.

Comparing and Contrasting

Have students compare and contrast the White House of 1801 with the White House of today. Have them contrast color, number of rooms in the main residence, comforts, additions, and so on. Ask students what has hardly changed.

Using Maps

1. On a map of the United States, find Washington, D.C. Show that it was in the approximate middle of the original thirteen colonies. Point them out. They were Connecticut, Delaware, Georgia, Maryland, Massachusetts, New Hampshire, New Jersey, New York, North Carolina, Pennsylvania, Rhode Island, South Carolina, and Virginia. Note that the area that is now Maine was once part of Massachusetts, and that West Virginia was once part of Virginia. Ask students which states the U.S. capital is closest to.

2. Have students point out the location of the state of Washington.

3. Look at a map of Washington, D.C., to see where the White House is in relation to other famous sites in the capital.

Discussion, Writing, or Research Topics

1. Have the class work as a team to list the U.S. presidents from FDR on in correct chronological order.

2. Have students read about some of the other interesting rooms in the White House besides those discussed in the reading. There are many excellent books about the White House. One is *Millie's Book: As Dictated to Barbara Bush*, edited by Lisa Drew, published in New York by William Morrow and Company, Incorporated in 1990. Another is *The White House: An Historic Guide*, 17th edition, edited by the White House Historical Association, published in 1991.

Extension Activities

Give students a list of questions about presidents. Have them work in research teams in the library to find the answers. The following is a list of suggested questions.

- Which president got married while serving in the White House? (Woodrow Wilson)
- Which president was shot and killed after only a few months in the White House? (James Garfield)
- Which president lost his bid for reelection and then won the presidency back in the following election? (Grover Cleveland)
- Which president served on the Supreme Court after he was president? (William Howard Taft)
- Which president had a daughter who married the grandson of an earlier president? (Richard Nixon)
- Which president had a sign on his desk that said, "The buck stops here"? (Harry Truman)
- Which president had a father who was also president? (John Quincy Adams)
- Which president had a cousin who had also been president? (Franklin D. Roosevelt)
- Which president's wife ran the government because the president had a stroke while in office? (Woodrow Wilson)

For ESL Students

1. Ask ESL students if anyone can visit the home of the leader of their native countries. Ask them if people ever protest outside the home. Compare and contrast American attitudes toward the head of the government and the attitudes common in their countries.

2. Discuss the way in which an American president and vice-president are selected. Most ESL students know nothing about electoral votes and find this very interesting.

READING COMPREHENSION

A. Mark each of these statements *True* or *False*.

_____ **1.** The president's office is a square room.

_____ **2.** Everything in the White House China Room was imported from China.

_____ **3.** An executive mansion is a very big house that a president or governor lives in while holding office.

_____ **4.** All of the U.S. presidents have lived in the White House except George Washington.

_____ **5.** James Hoban died soon after he designed the original White House.

B. What do the underlined phrases mean in this reading? Reread the paragraphs. Then circle the letter of the correct answer.

1. In paragraph 3, <u>everyone is welcome</u> means (a) they are all invited to come (b) each visit is appreciated.

2. In paragraph 4, <u>press conferences</u> means (a) meetings at which newspaper reporters and representatives of other media get information (b) very crowded meetings.

3. In paragraph 7, in the John Adams quotation, <u>but</u> means (a) however (b) except.

4. In paragraph 8, <u>first ladies</u> are (a) the wives of the presidents (b) female presidents of the United States.

5. In paragraph 12, <u>looked like</u> means (a) well-liked (b) resembled or looked similar to.

6. In paragraph 16, <u>about to</u> means (a) almost ready to (b) approximately.

7. In paragraph 22, <u>smoke-free</u> means (a) smoking isn't allowed (b) free cigarettes are given away to all visitors.

8. In paragraph 30, <u>points of view</u> means (a) opinions (b) anger.

BOOK 2

VOCABULARY PRACTICE

A. Say these words aloud. Then use some of them to complete the sentences that follow.

admire	foundation	oval	recycled
antique	imagine	payroll	require
attacked	installed	picketers	restoration
ceremony	mansion	protest	transparent

1. The _____ furniture in the White House is very valuable.

2. The president's office and the Blue Room are both _____ rooms.

3. There are millions of people on the government _____.

4. The ghost of Abraham Lincoln is _____. People said they could see through it.

5. When the British _____ Washington, D.C., they burned government buildings.

6. Can you _____ what it would be like to live in the White House?

7. Workers _____ indoor plumbing and central heating to modernize the White House.

8. The inauguration of a president is a very formal _____.

9. Picketers sometimes march in front of the White House to _____ government actions they don't like.

10. The White House is the most famous _____ in the United States.

B. Write the meanings of these phrases from the reading.

public housing (2) _____

crystal chandelier (4) _____

recycled tires (9) _____

private contributions (9) _____

bestseller (27) _____

ATTRACTIONS *Teacher's Guide*
© 1994 Contemporary Books
A Reproducible Exercise Page

HOMONYMS, SYNONYMS, AND SIMILAR WORDS

Discuss the similarities and differences between these pairs of words:

> hard / hardly   visitor / guest   whose / who's
> capital / Capitol   painting / portrait

Now use the words above to complete these sentences.

1. This _____ of my father is not a _____. It was drawn with colored chalk.

2. The mathematics test was very _____. I _____ got any of the answers right. Most of my answers were wrong.

3. Because you are a _____ to our city, I want you to be my _____ for dinner tonight.

4. The _____ building is in the nation's _____, Washington, D.C.

5. _____ going to be the next president? A woman _____ husband is president is often called the first lady.

BOOK 2

PARTS OF SPEECH AND INFLECTED FORMS

Complete these sentences using the correct noun form of the underlined verb. If necessary, use a dictionary for help.

Example: The people who <u>occupy</u> a room are its <u>occupants</u>.

1. When you <u>furnish</u> a room, you put _____ in it.

2. A person who <u>designs</u> something is a _____.

3. A person who <u>aids</u> (helps) someone in doing a job is sometimes called an _____.

4. They <u>added</u> a room to their home. They put on an _____.

5. The university <u>requires</u> students to take one semester of English composition. It is a _____.

WORD PARTS

A. Study the meanings of these word parts from the reading.

dis- = separate, reverse, take away or apart   *inter-* = between, among
ex-, *es-* = from, out, away from   *re-* = again, back
in- = not, inside   *un-* = not

Use some of the word parts above to complete the words in these sentences.

1. The _____terior of the White House is painted white.

2. The _____terior of the White House has a lot of antiques.

3. Anyone can visit the White House. No one is _____cluded.

4. Should we _____build this table and keep it, or should we _____card it (throw it away)?

5. There was an important meeting to discuss _____national peace.

6. In 1790, Washington, D.C., was an _____developed area.

7. Do you want formal or _____formal furniture?

B. Discuss the meaning of these compound words. Then answer the questions that follow.

    self-guided   smoke-free   worldwide   quarter-mile

1. *Self-* means "alone" or "without help." List two other compound words that contain *self-*.

   _____   _____

2. The ending *-free* means "without." List two other compound words that end with *-free*.

   _____   _____

3. *Worldwide* means "all over the world." What does *citywide* mean?

   _____

4. A *quarter-mile* track is about as long as how many blocks?

   _____

PHRASAL VERBS AND OTHER IDIOMS

Reread the paragraphs that these idioms are used in. The paragraph numbers are in parentheses. Then use some of the idioms to complete the sentences that follow. Put the idioms into an appropriate verb tense.

line up (3)	take place (9)	move into (14)	fall apart (20)
hang up (5)	look like (12)	call in (20)	put back (21)

1. Please _____ _____ and wait your turn.

2. Does your grandson _____ _____ your son?

3. The legs on this table are loose. You should fix them, or the table _____ _____ _____ completely.

4. Let's _____ _____ an electrician.

5. The accident _____ _____ near our home.

PATTERN PRACTICE

Jefferson didn't paint the White House himself. He hired someone to do it. The verb *have* **(or, informally,** *get***) followed by a noun or pronoun and past participle means that someone else did something for the subject.**

Examples: Jefferson <u>had</u> the White House <u>painted</u> white.
Next week, I'm <u>going to have</u> (or <u>get</u>) my hair <u>cut</u>.

Complete these statements. In the first blank, use *have* **or** *get* **in an appropriate tense. In the second blank, use an appropriate past participle.**

1. Tomorrow, I _____ my car _____.

2. These slacks were too long, so I _____ them _____.
(Use the past participle of *shorten*.)

3. Our TV set isn't working. Call the repairman and _____ it _____.

4. I went to the dentist, and I _____ my teeth _____.

BOOK 2

PHONICS AND PRONUNCIATION

A. Circle the silent letters in these words.

building	design	guest	plumbing
business	folk	guided	through
daughter	foreign	honest	well-known

B. Form the plurals of most (but not all) nouns that end in *f* or *fe* by changing the *f* to *v* and adding *es*. Read these words aloud. Then say their plurals. Then write their plurals on the blank lines. Use a dictionary for help, if necessary.

chief _____   roof _____

knife _____   shelf _____

life _____   wife _____

C. The *ch* at the beginning of *chandelier* sounds like *sh*. Read these phrases aloud, and circle all the *sh* sounds.

special occasion	laundry chute	a mansion in Michigan
the Pacific Ocean	a social event	expensive machinery

D. Say these words aloud. Notice that their last syllables sound the same. Circle the last syllable of each word.

million   union

JAZZ CITY

(PAGES 31–41)

Pre-Reading Activities

Discussion Questions

1. About New Orleans: What do you think of when you hear the name New Orleans? What are some things the city is famous for? (List the answers on the board.) Do you think all of these will be discussed in this selection?

2. About voodoo: Where did this religion come from? What were some of the practices associated with it? Is it a major religion today?

3. About Lent: What does this period mean to Christians? How is Mardi Gras related to Easter? Has anyone in the class ever been to a Mardi Gras celebration in New Orleans or elsewhere? (Note that the idea is to have a short period of self-indulgence before a long period of self-denial.) Is this a good idea? Or do people get too wild and destructive?

4. About jazz: What is jazz? What is its connection with New Orleans? Why are Americans proud of jazz? Is jazz "black music"? What famous jazz musicians do you know of?

5. About the teaser: What three countries' flags flew over New Orleans in the early 1800s? (The answer is in paragraph 12—Spanish, French, and American flags.)

Section Headings

"A Fight for Control": Ask students what was being fought over. The fight was over control of the Mississippi River, the longest river in North America.

"Water, Water Everywhere . . .": This is a quotation from a poem titled "The Rime of the Ancient Mariner" by Samuel Taylor Coleridge. Students might enjoy reading the part with quote "Water, water everywhere / Nor any drop to drink." This quote can also describe what is a very common situation during severe floods, when a community's drinking water may get contaminated.

Important Vocabulary from the Reading

1. Discuss the following words related to the geography and climate of New Orleans: *crescent, port, swamp, flood*.

2. Discuss the meanings of words relating to structures including *levees* and *causeway*.

3. Discuss words relating to ethnicity and immigration including *Cajun, Creole, assimilation, voodoo*, and *descendants*.

4. Discuss the meaning of the word *improvise* as it relates to jazz and to other art forms, such as dance. Also point out that a person can improvise in any field of endeavor.

Activities to Accompany the Reading

Playing Word Games

Have students scan the reading (including Sidelights) in search of all the nicknames for New Orleans. They should find five. Four are in paragraph 1 and the fifth is in Sidelights. In addition, in the mid-19th century, New Orleans was called Paris in America because all kinds of cultural events in different languages took place there. Even today, the French Quarter is considered the most European-looking area in the United States.

Students can also list the nicknames for the Mississippi River, such as the Big Muddy, Old Man River, and the Mighty Mississippi.

Improvising Scenes

1. Have one student play the role of Jean Laffitte, who is approached by the British and the Americans, both seeking his help in the Battle of New Orleans.

2. Have students play the roles of tourists walking around the French Quarter, pointing out the sights to one another.

Comparing and Contrasting

Compare and contrast with students New Orleans as it was in 1722 with New Orleans as it is today. Compare the ethnic groups living there, the types of architecture, and the likelihood of problems with flooding.

Using Maps

1. On a map of North and South America, find the following: New Orleans, the Gulf of Mexico, the Mississippi River, the Great Lakes, the Pacific Ocean, the Atlantic Ocean, Canada, and Nova Scotia. Also find the Caribbean Sea and the West Indies. Point out the borders between North America, Central America, and South America. Show students the area that was the Louisiana Territory on a historical map, if one is available.

2. On a map of the world, find the continent of Europe and the countries France, Spain, and Germany. Be sure that students know what continents are in the Eastern Hemisphere and which are in the Western Hemisphere. Also, be sure they understand the difference between England and Great Britain.

Discussion, Writing, or Research Topics

1. Every year, about 700 conventions come to New Orleans. Ask students the following: What is a convention? What are some different kinds? Why is New Orleans such a popular choice for conventions? What other American cities also enjoy a large convention business?

2. Many religions have a period of self-denial similar to Lent. Ask students if they've ever given up some pleasure, comfort, type of behavior, or food as part of religious practice.

3. Have students look up Easter in an encyclopedia to find out how its date is determined.

Extension Activities

1. Have students find some Cajun or Creole recipes to read in class. Ask if the ingredients sound strange to them. If possible, try to share some Cajun and/or Creole food with the class, either at a restaurant or by having students prepare a meal themselves.

2. Listen with the class to some jazz recordings, especially New Orleans–style jazz in the tradition of Louis Armstrong. Point out that jazz has influenced popular and classical music so that jazz elements are in modern ballet and even in symphonic music. The music of George Gershwin and Leonard Bernstein contains many elements of jazz. Some students may have favorite jazz artists whose work they'd like to share with the class by bringing in recordings.

3. Read aloud some sections of Henry Wadsworth Longfellow's long narrative poem "Evangeline." It tells the tragic story of two Acadian lovers, Evangeline and Gabriel, who are separated when exiled from Nova Scotia. They both travel down the Mississippi River to Louisiana but keep missing each other. They finally find each other when Gabriel is an old man dying in a poorhouse.

For ESL Students

This chapter provides a good opportunity to teach the English names of many countries and the names of the languages spoken in these countries.

1. Begin with the names mentioned in the reading: England, Germany, France, and Spain. Have students point out on the map each of these countries. Then have them write and pronounce the names of the languages.

2. Make a list of the countries that the students in the class come from. Then list the language(s) spoken in each country.

3. Ask students the following: What languages are spoken in Canada? What languages are spoken in the countries of Central and South America? (Note that the language of Brazil is Portuguese, not Spanish. Note that French is the native language of Haiti.)

READING COMPREHENSION

A. Mark each of these statements *True* or *False*.

_____ 1. Because New Orleans is an old city, it doesn't have modern skyscrapers.

_____ 2. The Cajuns spoke French because they came from France.

_____ 3. The French Quarter in New Orleans has mostly French architecture.

_____ 4. The U.S. government bought the Louisiana Territory from France.

_____ 5. Every year, the city of New Orleans spends millions of dollars on its Mardi Gras festival.

_____ 6. The cities of the dead are cemeteries.

_____ 7. New Orleans has a population of about a half-million people.

B. Scan the reading to find answers to these questions. Then write a short answer to each question.

1. Who was Louisiana named after? _____

2. Who named Louisiana? _____

3. What country did the Cajuns come from? _____

4. What military leader won the Battle of New Orleans in 1814?

_____

5. What river curves around the French Quarter? _____

C. Mark each statement *F* if it is a fact and *O* if it is an opinion.

_____ 1. New Orleans is a great vacation spot.

_____ 2. The Mississippi River curves around the French Quarter.

_____ 3. Jack Laffitte was a great American.

_____ 4. New Orleans's Mardi Gras is too crowded to be fun.

BOOK 2

VOCABULARY PRACTICE

Say these words aloud. Then use them to complete the sentences that follow.

alter	carnival	entire	preserve
authentic	causeway	improvising	unlikely
balcony	crescent	pirate	voodoo

1. The _____ of an apartment is outdoors, but the one in a theater is indoors.

2. New Orleans is called the _____ City because the original city (where the French Quarter is now located) was built along a bend in the Mississippi River.

3. We didn't have time to see the _____ French Quarter, but we saw most of it.

4. A _____ steals treasures from ships.

5. Is that musician reading music, or is he _____?

6. Mardi Gras is a _____.

7. _____ is a religion that combines African and Caribbean religious beliefs with ideas and symbols from Christianity.

8. The residents of New Orleans want to _____ the historic buildings in the French Quarter.

9. New Orleans residents don't want anyone to _____ the outside of the buildings in the French Quarter.

10. It's _____ that the city of New Orleans will ever tear down the French Quarter.

11. In the French Quarter, visitors see _____ 18th-century buildings.

12. A _____ is a bridge over water.

ATTRACTIONS *Teacher's Guide*
© 1994 Contemporary Books
A Reproducible Exercise Page

HOMONYMS, SYNONYMS, AND SIMILAR WORDS

A. Match each word in the column on the left with the word or phrase that means nearly the same in the column on the right. Write the correct letters on the blank lines.

_____ **1.** alter   **(a)** learning

_____ **2.** bury   **(b)** recognize

_____ **3.** causeway   **(c)** change

_____ **4.** curve   **(d)** complete, all, whole

_____ **5.** entire   **(e)** inter, put underground

_____ **6.** identify   **(f)** promise

_____ **7.** knowledge   **(g)** bridge

_____ **8.** swear   **(h)** bend

B. Circle the word that best completes each sentence.

1. Most of New Orleans is below (sea, see) level.

2. Did the dog (bury, berry) the bone in the garden?

3. Did you (altar, alter) your plans and cancel your vacation?

PARTS OF SPEECH AND INFLECTED FORMS

Write a noun form of each verb listed. Use the reading or a dictionary for help.

1. believe _____

5. grow _____

2. bury _____

6. improvise _____

3. deny _____

7. know _____

4. entertain _____

8. valuable _____

BOOK 2

WORD PARTS

Look these words up in an unabridged American English dictionary. Then answer the questions.

carnival   improvise

1. What language did the word come
   from?

   _____

4. What language did the word come
   from?

   _____

2. What do the two word parts mean?

   _____ _____

5. What do the two word parts mean?

   _____ _____

3. What does the word mean today?

   _____

   _____

6. What does the word mean today?

   _____

   _____

PHRASAL VERBS AND OTHER IDIOMS

Reread the paragraphs that these idioms are used in. The paragraph numbers are in parentheses. Then use the idioms to complete the sentences that follow.

sea level (1)   get the ball rolling (2)   warm welcome (9)
turn into (2)   (be) in for a big surprise (9)

1. Can we _____ this apartment _____ a nice home?

2. Let's get started. Let's _____.

3. When I came to this city, I got a _____ from my friends and
   relatives. They gave a big party for me.

4. Mexico City is about a mile above _____, so some tourists feel
   dizzy there.

5. If you really believe I'm going to lend you $500, you are _____

   _____.

ATTRACTIONS *Teacher's Guide*
© 1994 Contemporary Books
A Reproducible Exercise Page

PATTERN PRACTICE

A. Read each statement. Then, after the word *but* or the word *however*, write a contrasting idea. You will find information for the contrasting idea in the reading in the paragraph indicated.

1. In the Battle of New Orleans, Andrew Jackson had fewer soldiers than the British did. But _____. (14, 15)

2. The Battle of New Orleans was a great victory for Andrew Jackson. But
    _____. (16)

3. Water used to create many problems for the city of New Orleans, but
    _____. (17)

4. Some people call Mardi Gras "the greatest free show on earth." However,
    _____. (25)

5. At one time, New Orleans was considered a good place for adults to vacation, but today _____. (26)

B. In paragraph 3, *moreover* is used to connect two reasons why New Orleans was a good location for a city. What were these reasons?

_____

_____

C. After each statement, write an additional idea after *moreover*.

1. New Orleans is a wonderful city to visit because it has many fine restaurants. Moreover, _____.

2. New Orleans is an important seaport because of its location. First of all, it's located on the Mississippi River. Moreover, _____
    _____.

BOOK 2

PHONICS AND PRONUNCIATION

A. The sound *ur* is spelled many different ways. Read these words aloud. Then circle the letters that spell the *ur* sound.

bird	curve	heard	settler	word
birth	earn	leader	surprise	world
culture	first	learn	transfer	worst

B. List the common spellings for the sound *ur*.

_____

C. Read the following words aloud. Then circle the silent letter(s) in each word.

bisque	huge	sausage
descend	Mardi Gras	sign
highland	pleasant	spread
hour	rhythm	value

D. Do these pairs of words sound the same? If they are homonyms, write *Yes* on the blank line. If not, write *No*.

1. descent / decent _____

2. hours / ours _____

3. huge / hug _____

4. rhythm / rhyme _____

ATTRACTIONS *Teacher's Guide*
© 1994 Contemporary Books
A Reproducible Exercise Page

GOLDEN GATE

(PAGES 45–55)

Pre-Reading Activities

Discussion Questions

1. About California: Where is California? What do you know about the state? What is it well known for? Is the climate the same in northern California and southern California?

2. About Alcatraz: Why was it a good idea to build a maximum-security prison on an island? Were there any problems with having it on an island?

3. About two points of entry: The main place for European immigrants to enter the United States in earlier years was Ellis Island in New York. Many more people came from Europe during that time than from Asia. In fact, Chinese immigration was limited for a long time. Many immigrants from the Far East entered the country via Angel Island, near San Francisco. Why do the two ports of entry for U.S. immigration make geographical sense?

4. About islands: Would you like to live on an island? What is appealing about islands? What is forbidding? Can you think of books, movies, or TV shows set on islands? What are they?

5. About the idea of privilege: Prisoners at Alcatraz had to earn family visits, books, radios, recreation, and jobs. For a free citizen, are these things rights or privileges? Do you think it's a good idea to have people earn privileges like these in prison?

6. About the teaser: What does Alcatraz mean? (The bird the teaser refers to is the pelican. Another bird, referred to later, is the Birdman of Alcatraz. Sometimes people in prison are also referred to as *jailbirds*, a slang term for inmates. *Strange birds*, meaning odd people, is also related to the meaning of the teaser.)

Section Headings

"The Rock": Ask students the following: Why might Alcatraz be described as the Rock? What is the main characteristic of a rock?

"From Lighthouse to Prison": This heading reveals that before it became a prison, Alcatraz Island was the site of the West Coast's first lighthouse.

"A National Park": This subhead suggests that after Alcatraz closed, it became a recreational area.

"Triangle in the Bay": This heading signals a different topic, a triangular island near Alcatraz Island. The size of the type of the heading means a separate topic.

"Wartime Use": This subhead indicates that the wartime uses of Angel Island will be presented.

Important Vocabulary from the Reading

1. Discuss some Alcatraz vocabulary: *maximum security, minimum privilege, gangster, Prohibition, regulations, reward,* and *solitary confinement*.

2. Define and discuss *right* versus *privilege, maximum security* versus *minimum security*.

3. Discuss words relating to the Golden Gate Bridge: *span, split, arches, x-braces,* and *architect*.

Activities to Accompany the Reading

Playing Word Games

1. Have students find all the names of plants and animals in the reading.

2. Define a nickname. Have students find all the nicknames in the reading. Ask students the following: What is a nickname for San Francisco? (City of Golden Dreams). Do any of you have a nickname? What is it?

Improvising Scenes

1. Tell students they are Native Americans claiming Alcatraz for themselves. Have them tell a reporter why the island should be a Native American cultural center.

2. Tell students they are Chinese immigrants on Angel Island. Have them each tell a brief story about why he or she is homesick.

Summarizing Chronology

Have students summarize the history of Angel Island. Have them make a time line of important events on the island.

Comparing and Contrasting

Have students compare and contrast (orally or in writing) Alcatraz and Angel Island.

Using Maps

1. Point out California on a map of the United States. Then have students find San Francisco. Have them locate Alcatraz and Angel Island, off the coast of San Francisco. On a map of San Francisco, have them find the Golden Gate Bridge and Fort Mason.

2. On a map of the world, have students find other places mentioned in the reading: Spain, Japan, the Philippines, Australia, Portugal, the Panama Canal, and Hawaii.

Studying Word Parts to Build Vocabulary

Discuss the prefix *pro-* in *prohibition*, *dis-* in *discovered*, and *em-* in *embarkation*.

Discussion, Writing, or Research Topics

Have students select one of the following topics, do library research on it, and then work with classmates to prepare a group presentation for the class.

- Alcatraz, the federal prison
- Fort Mason
- Golden Gate Bridge
- the Coast Miwok Indians
- Juan Manuel de Ayala
- the California Gold Rush
- Chinese immigration to California
- Al Capone
- Robert Stroud, Birdman of Alcatraz
- famous escape attempts from Alcatraz
- Native American occupation of Alcatraz

Extension Activities

1. You might use photographs of San Francisco, of Alcatraz, or of Angel Island or travel videos to introduce students to the sites described in the story.

2. Gangsters who were incarcerated at Alcatraz are the subject of many popular Hollywood films. Have students watch one of the many films on this subject or one about Alcatraz in particular; *Escape from Alcatraz* or *Birdman of Alcatraz*.

For ESL Students

To help ESL students develop listening skills and practice verbs, ask the following questions. Encourage students to use full sentences when responding.

- When did the prison on Alcatraz close?
- When was the United States having a lot of trouble with gangsters?
- Did prisoners in Alcatraz have many privileges?
- Who is the most famous prisoner of Alcatraz?
- What are canaries?
- Were women ever prisoners at Alcatraz?
- When was gold discovered in California?
- What color is the Golden Gate Bridge?
- Is Angel Island smaller or larger than Alcatraz?
- What are barracks?
- How were some wildflowers planted on Angel Island?

READING COMPREHENSION

A. Mark each of these statements *True* or *False*.

_____ **1.** Alcatraz was always a federal prison.

_____ **2.** The Confederate Army never attacked San Francisco Bay.

_____ **3.** Not all prisoners were allowed to read books.

_____ **4.** Salmon spawned near Angel Island.

_____ **5.** Only native trees and flowers grow on Angel Island.

_____ **6.** Soldiers leaving for the Pacific saw a 60-foot Good-bye sign on Angel Island.

_____ **7.** Today, the federal government funds Angel Island.

_____ **8.** A tourist couldn't see a bear on Angel Island.

B. What does each word mean in the paragraph indicated? Reread the paragraphs. Then circle the letter of the correct answer.

1. maximum (1): (a) the highest amount (b) the lowest amount

2. necessities (4): (a) essentials (b) luxuries

3. attempts (5): (a) tries (b) successes

4. solitary (7): (a) with others (b) alone

5. raid (9): (a) attack (b) visit

6. architect (15): (a) person who designs structures (b) person who visits theaters

7. immigrants (17): (a) people leaving the country they've lived in (b) people coming to live in a new place

8. disputed (21): (a) agreed with (b) argued against

BOOK 2

VOCABULARY PRACTICE

A. Say these vocabulary words aloud. Then use some of them to complete the sentences that follow.

convicts	embarkation	featured	published
counterfeiting	exotic	foghorns	solitary
denied	expensive	pelicans	spawned

1. Thirty _____ warn ships in the harbor.

2. _____ is illegal in the United States.

3. Prisoners were _____ family visits, except as rewards.

4. Salmon _____ each year in Raccoon Strait.

5. Angel Island was also an _____ point for soldiers in World War II.

6. The Chinese poems written on Angel Island were _____.

7. Sometimes veterans brought _____ plants back from foreign countries.

8. Finally, it was too _____ to renovate Alcatraz.

B. Match each word in the column on the left with its opposite in the column on the right. Write the correct letters on the blank lines.

_____ 1. boring   **(a)** temporarily

_____ 2. common   **(b)** island

_____ 3. disobeyed   **(c)** cheap

_____ 4. expensive   **(d)** rare

_____ 5. forever   **(e)** landowners

_____ 6. mainland   **(f)** minded

_____ 7. reward   **(g)** punishment

_____ 8. squatters   **(h)** interesting

ATTRACTIONS *Teacher's Guide*
© 1994 Contemporary Books
A Reproducible Exercise Page

HOMONYMS, SYNONYMS, AND SIMILAR WORDS

A. Using these pairs of homonyms, complete the sentences that follow.

passed / past   urn / earn   sells / cells

1. The Chinese immigrants _____ many weeks on Angel Island. This happened in the _____.

2. You had to _____ rewards in Alcatraz. He kept his money hidden in an _____.

3. During the day, prisoners stayed in their _____. He _____ souvenirs of Alcatraz at a store in San Francisco.

B. Match each word in the column on the left with the correct word or phrase from the column on the right. Write the correct letters on the blank lines.

_____ 1. alongside		**(a)** temporary housing, building for soldiers
_____ 2. confinement		**(b)** rules
_____ 3. deserted		**(c)** imprisonment
_____ 4. barracks		**(d)** abandoned
_____ 5. regulations		**(e)** Alcatraz
_____ 6. depression		**(f)** stay
_____ 7. remain		**(g)** next to
_____ 8. spawn		**(h)** lay eggs
_____ 9. The Rock		**(i)** difficulty
_____ 10. trouble		**(j)** bad economic period

BOOK 2

PARTS OF SPEECH AND INFLECTED FORMS

A. Complete the sentences below with an adjective formed from the participle (*-ing* word) form of the underlined word.

1. Prisoners tried to <u>escape</u>. _____ prisoners were often caught.

2. Prisoners were often <u>bored</u> at Alcatraz. _____ prison life was meant to teach them a lesson.

3. Birds <u>nested</u> on Alcatraz. Strange _____ birds gave the island its name.

4. Musicians <u>performed</u> the foghorn concerto. The _____ musicians played music all night.

5. The Golden Gate Bridge is <u>arched</u>. The _____ bridge is one of the most beautiful on Earth.

6. Salmon <u>spawned</u> near Angel Island. _____ salmon were easy to catch.

B. Change from active to passive constructions.

1. Prisoners built the cellblocks. The cellblocks _____ by prisoners.

2. Architects designed the bridge. The bridge _____ by architects.

3. Gangsters inhabited the prison. The prison _____ by gangsters.

4. Salmon laid their eggs. Eggs _____ by salmon.

5. Hollywood made many movies about Alcatraz. Many movies about Alcatraz _____ in Hollywood.

6. In 1859, the U.S. government began to use the fort to protect San Francisco Bay. The fort _____ to protect the bay.

7. In 1848, some people discovered gold near San Francisco. In 1848, gold _____ near San Francisco.

ATTRACTIONS *Teacher's Guide*
© 1994 Contemporary Books
A Reproducible Exercise Page

WORD PARTS

Use some of these words with suffixes to complete the sentences that follow.

confinement   government   residence
education   plentiful   squatters
equipment   recreational

1. Solitary _____ was used as punishment.

2. _____ and training were not available to Alcatraz prisoners.

3. The _____ built the first lighthouse on the West Coast in 1859.

4. A huge _____ area contains Fort Mason, Alcatraz, and many other sights.

5. Wildlife is _____ on Angel Island.

PHRASAL VERBS AND OTHER IDIOMS

Reread the paragraphs that the idioms in the column on the left are used in. Then match each idiom with its definition in the column on the right. Write the correct letters on the blank lines.

_____ **1.** keep running (1)   **(a)** stopped operating

_____ **2.** closed its doors (1)   **(b)** a number of

_____ **3.** hard time (4)   **(c)** continue operating

_____ **4.** earn through (4)   **(d)** publicize

_____ **5.** make known (13)   **(e)** gain something by

_____ **6.** pocketful of (20)   **(f)** confinement without privileges

PATTERN PRACTICE

A. Connect these pairs of sentences by inserting a comma plus *and* or *but*, whichever is appropriate.

Example: Some people thought that Alcatraz prisoners should not be educated. Others believed they should be trained.

<u>Some people thought that Alcatraz prisoners should not be educated, but others believed they should be trained.</u>

1. Fish could be caught on the island. Deer were also plentiful there.

_____

2. Some Chinese immigrants were hopeful. Other Chinese immigrants were fearful.

_____

3. The veterans came home from the Pacific. They saw the Welcome Home sign.

_____

4. People want a museum on Angel Island. There isn't enough money to build a museum.

_____

B. Connect these sentences by inserting a comma plus *and* or *or*, whichever is appropriate.

1. Prisoners could cooperate. They could stay in solitary confinement.

_____

2. Reading books was a reward. A family visit was a reward.

_____

3. The building could be fixed. It could be torn down.

_____

4. Some people prefer to ride the ferry. Others take private boats.

_____

ATTRACTIONS *Teacher's Guide*
© 1994 Contemporary Books
A Reproducible Exercise Page

A WALL OF NAMES

(PAGES 59–69)

Pre-Reading Activities

Discussion Questions

1. About the Vietnam War: What do you know about this war and American reaction to it in the 1960s and early 1970s? Have you seen any movies about this war? Did you know anyone who was killed in Vietnam?

2. Predicting content: What questions about the Vietnam War do you think the text will answer? (Have students jot them down, and suggest they look for the answers as they read.)

3. Guessing statistics: How many Americans do you think fought in Vietnam? What was the average age of Americans serving in Vietnam? (The answer is on the Sidelights page.)

4. About the Wall: Based on the photograph on page 61, which letter of the alphabet does it resemble? Do you think that similarity was intentional? How many names do you think are on the Wall? What military personnel were/are eligible to be listed? What symbols are used after the names?

5. About visiting the Wall: Have you ever been there? If so, describe the setting. What did you see there? What did you notice about the other visitors? What did they leave at the Wall?

6. About the teaser: (Explain to students that when Maya Lin's design was first printed in newspapers and magazines around the country, there were many negative reactions.) Do you think that, because the winner was a woman, quite young, and still a student, people found it easy to find fault? Does Lin's Wall glamorize war and make it heroic? (Paragraph 9 addresses this issue.)

Section Headings

"The Wall That Remembers": This heading is figurative. Ask students to restate the idea in literal language. (The Wall serves as a reminder to help people remember.)

Important Vocabulary from the Reading

1. Discuss the noun *controversy* and the adjective *controversial*. Then the class may compile a list of words beginning with *contro-* and *contra-*, which mean "against" or "opposite." These include *contradict*, *contraband*, *contraceptive*, *contrary*, and *contrast*.

2. The reading contains several words associated with the military and military conflict, which students may discuss. These include *veteran*, *infantrymen*, and *surrender*. Words about tragedies often associated with war include *wounded*, *disabled*, *missing*, *tragedy*, *casualties*, and *sacrifice*. The students may also discuss the various branches of the American military—army, navy, marines, air force, coast guard—and the particular responsibilities of each.

3. The reading includes some words related to remembering and reminders, which students may discuss. These are *memorial*, *memorable*, and *memento*.

4. Discuss the word *criticism*, which is used in this reading to mean negative reaction to something, pointing out what's wrong with it. But students should be reminded that *criticism* also means analysis and evaluation. It can be negative or positive. A movie critic, for example, might find a movie praiseworthy.

Activities to Accompany the Reading

Playing Word Games

This game should be played in teams of two or three and without a dictionary. Set a time limit (perhaps 10 minutes). Students must create noun-verb pairs or noun-adjective pairs from the vocabulary in the reading. At least one of the words in each pair must be in the selection. Here are some examples:

death/dead
tragedy/tragic
controversy/controversial
sacrifice/sacrificial
darkness/dark

Improvising Scenes

1. Have students role-play two people at the Wall arguing. One thinks it is a suitable memorial, and the other person hates it.

2. Have students role-play being the statues near the Wall coming to life and having a conversation about the visitors who come to the Wall.

Summarizing

Have students summarize in chronological order the development of the Vietnam Veterans Memorial—the Wall plus the added sculptures.

Using Maps

1. Look at a map of the city of Washington, D.C., that has the major sites on it. Point out the White House, the Wall, and the sites mentioned in Sidelights.

2. Point out Vietnam on a map of the world.

Discussion, Writing, or Research Topics

1. Do you think Jan Scruggs is satisfied with the outcome of his brainstorm? Why or why not?

2. Have students look up one of the people or sites listed below in a periodicals index and find a recent article about the person or place. They should then prepare a one-paragraph abstract of the article.

People	Places
Maya Lin	Washington, D.C.
Frederick Hart	Vietnam
Oliver Stone	

Extension Activities

1. Discuss with students the advantages and disadvantages of a military career. If possible, have some speakers come in to talk about this to the class.

2. Listen to recordings of some of the 1960s protest songs, for example, those written and sung by Joan Baez.

3. Suggest that the class see a movie about the Vietnam War or about the experiences of veterans of that war. The movie that Jan Scruggs saw the night he had his brainstorm about a memorial was the 1978 film *The Deer Hunter*. Show some or all of this film in class or suggest that students rent the videotape and watch it at home. Another movie set in Vietnam and available on videotape is Oliver Stone's 1986 film *Platoon*. It won Oscars for best picture and best directing.

4. Read excerpts to the class from *Paco's Story* by Larry Heineman. This short novel tells about a man haunted by his memories of Vietnam.

5. Students may enjoy learning about another impressive war memorial, the one that honors the nation's first African-American regiment, the 54th, led by Colonel Robert Gould Shaw. This regiment of inexperienced soldiers fought heroically in the Civil War. The 1989 movie *Glory* tells their story. Further information about the regiment (and a photograph of it) is in the U.S. Government Printing Office pamphlet "Black Heritage Trail" (1992-0-601-783). The Robert Gould Shaw and 54th Regiment Memorial, a high-relief bronze sculpture, is in Boston.

For ESL Students

1. The reading mentions that Maya Lin was a college senior when she won the design competition. Be sure that ESL students know the names for the four years of high school and college: *freshman*, *sophomore*, *junior*, and *senior*.

2. On your classroom chalkboard, draw these shapes discussed in the reading: circle, cross or plus sign, and diamond. Then add these common shapes: square, rectangle, triangle, and oval. Be sure that students know the English names of these shapes. Also, have students name some common three-dimensional shapes, such as a sphere, cube, and cylinder.

3. Show pictures of a hawk and a dove. Discuss the traits of these birds that make them appropriate symbols of war and peace.

READING COMPREHENSION

A. Mark each of these statements *True* or *False*.

_____ **1.** The American government paid for the Vietnam Veterans Memorial.

_____ **2.** The Vietnam Veterans Memorial is in Vietnam.

_____ **3.** The total number of American casualties from the Vietnam War was about 58,000.

_____ **4.** Diane Evans was a Vietnam vet.

_____ **5.** Both the Vietnam Veterans Memorial and the Vietnam Women's Memorial were designed by women.

B. Answer these questions about the reading in complete sentences.

1. What information in paragraph 1 proves that the Vietnam Veterans Memorial is popular with tourists?

_____

2. Why didn't Americans cheer when the military men and women came home from Vietnam?

_____

3. Why did Jan Scruggs want a memorial for Vietnam veterans?

_____

4. What does the Wall reflect?

_____

5. What does the Wall make people reflect about?

_____

READING COMPREHENSION (CONTINUED)

C. What does each word or phrase mean in the paragraph indicated? Reread the paragraphs. Then circle the letter of the correct answer.

1. <u>veterans</u> (1): (a) career military personnel (b) people that were in the military in the past

2. <u>brainstorm</u> (5): (a) a headache (b) a very good idea

3. <u>unanimous</u> (8): (a) half (b) all

4. <u>news media</u> (9): (a) people who are in the news a lot (b) newspapers, magazines, TV, and radio

5. <u>a sufficient tribute</u> (9): (a) enough of an honor (b) an insult

6. <u>criticism</u> (10): (a) insults (b) praise

7. <u>eligible</u> (15): (a) qualified to do something (b) desiring to do something

8. <u>heartrending</u> (22): (a) controversial (b) causing great sadness

D. Number these statements 1–8 in the order that they occurred, beginning with the earliest. Scan the reading to find the dates you need.

_____ The U.S. military pulled out of Vietnam.

_____ Jan Scruggs raised $8 million to create a memorial.

_____ Diane Carlson served in Vietnam.

_____ The sculpture of three women and a wounded soldier was placed near the Wall.

_____ Maya Lin won a design competition.

_____ The Vietnam Veterans Memorial celebrated its 10th anniversary.

_____ The statue of three infantrymen was added to the Vietnam Veterans Memorial.

_____ At this time, there were 58,183 names on the Wall.

VOCABULARY PRACTICE

A. Say these words aloud. Then use some of them to complete the sentences that follow.

casualties	donation	protest	surrender
compromise	monument	sacrifice	unanimous
disabled	parade	sculptor	wounded

1. I wanted to spend $1,000 on our vacation. My husband said we should spend only $500. So we're going to _____ and spend $750.

2. Millions of people were killed or wounded in the Vietnam War. There were a lot of _____.

3. When Americans disagree with actions of their government, they often _____ against policies they dislike.

4. When you give money to a good cause, you are making a _____ or a contribution to that cause.

5. A soldier who is killed, _____, or _____ in battle is a casualty of a war.

6. A _____ designed the statue near the Wall.

7. Veterans march in a _____ on Veterans Day.

8. There was no controversy about the matter. The club members were _____ in their decision.

B. Of the 12 words listed in Part A above, list four that are commonly used to talk about war or how war affects people.

_____   _____

_____   _____

HOMONYMS, SYNONYMS, AND SIMILAR WORDS

A. Read these sentences aloud. Notice the differences in pronunciation, spelling, and meaning between the underlined words in each pair of sentences.

The movie star was <u>surrounded</u> by a crowd of people.

The soldiers dropped their guns and <u>surrendered</u>.

Wear <u>casual</u> clothes, even blue jeans.

The <u>casualties</u> of a war include people killed and wounded.

B. In a dictionary, look up the meanings of these two pairs of homonyms. Write a definition for each word.

capital / Capitol   morning / mourning

1. capital: _____

2. Capitol: _____

3. morning: _____

4. mourning: _____

C. Look up the meanings of *disabled* and *wounded*. Write a definition for each word.

1. disabled: _____

2. wounded: _____

D. Complete these sentences using some of the words from Parts A, B, and C above.

1. Washington, D.C., is the _____ of the United States.

2. The _____ in Washington, D.C., is a white building with a golden dome. Congress meets there.

3. He was shot in the arm and _____, but he's fine now.

4. This is a photograph of my grandmother _____ by her 14 grandchildren. (They are standing around her.)

5. They are _____ the death of their daughter.

ATTRACTIONS *Teacher's Guide*
© 1994 Contemporary Books
A Reproducible Exercise Page

PARTS OF SPEECH AND INFLECTED FORMS

A. These words can be nouns or verbs.

      compromise   design   sacrifice   surrender

Use them in these sentences. Add past-tense or plural endings when needed.

1. People make a lot of _____ for their children.

2. Who _____ the Vietnam Veterans Memorial?

3. Maya Lin won the competition with a simple _____.

4. In a good marriage, the husband and wife make a lot of _____ to reach an agreement.

5. In 1975, South Vietnam _____, and the war ended.

B. Use these words to complete the sentences that follow.

remember (verb)   memorable (adjective)   memory, memorial, memento (nouns)

1. This medal is a _____ of my years in the army.

2. The Vietnam Veterans _____ helps people _____ those who have died.

3. What was the most _____ day of your life?

4. Do you have a good _____? Can you _____ facts?

C. The word *miss* and its inflected forms can have different meanings. Read these sentences. Then identify what part of speech the word is in each sentence (noun, verb, or adjective).

1. My dog died last week. I <u>miss</u> him a lot. _____

2. I ran as fast as I could, but I <u>missed</u> the bus. _____

3. My <u>missing</u> sweater was in Joe's car. _____

4. The title <u>Miss</u> refers to an unmarried woman. _____

5. "A <u>miss</u> is as good as a mile" is an old saying. _____

WORD PARTS

Study the meanings of these word parts from the reading. Then use some of them to complete the words in the sentences that follow.

com- = together, with
contra-, *contro-* = against, opposite
in- = in, into, no, not
non-, *dis-*, *im-* = not

inter- = between, among
-less = without
memor- = remembering

1. He is _____abled because of serious war injuries.

2. It's _____possible to remember everything you learn.

3. The names are _____scribed on the Wall.

4. That movie was very boring, so it seemed end_____.

5. When someone tells you that you're wrong, that person has _____dicted you.

PHRASAL VERBS AND OTHER IDIOMS

Reread the paragraphs these idioms are used in. The paragraph numbers are in parentheses. Then use some of the idioms to answer the questions that follow.

drag on (3)
on and on (3)

come back (5)
middle of the night (5)

run (a business, etc.) (5)
be made of (11)

1. What happened to Jan Scruggs in the middle of the night?

   _____

2. For how long did the Vietnam War drag on and on?

   _____

3. Why didn't some people come back from the war?

   _____

4. What organization did Scruggs run? _____

5. What is the Wall made of? _____

ATTRACTIONS *Teacher's Guide*
© 1994 Contemporary Books
A Reproducible Exercise Page

A RICH PORT

(PAGES 73–81)

Pre-Reading Activities

Discussion Questions

1. About islands: Has anyone ever lived on an island? How is living on an island different from living on the mainland? Do people think of islands as more primitive and isolated? Is this accurate? (Remind students that New York City and Japan are islands.)

2. About New World exploration: Why did explorers from Spain go to the Caribbean?

3. About Puerto Rico: (It is a member of a group of islands called the Greater Antilles. The Greater Antilles makes up the easternmost part of the island group called the West Indies. Seven thousand smaller islands, mostly uninhabited, surround Puerto Rico.) Has anyone ever visited the West Indies? Why are they called the West Indies?

4. About Old San Juan: What other cities have historic districts? What can be learned from looking at old churches, forts, and government buildings? Why did building a walled city make sense?

5. About the teaser: When might baseball have first been played in Puerto Rico? (The answer is on page 79. Discuss native cultures and games. You might mention other cultures in which sporting events were connected to religious celebrations and pageants; such as Mayan, Greek, and Roman. Asian practices like judo also connect a philosophy of life to physical activity.)

Section Headings

Ask students the following questions regarding the headings and subheads:

"A Perfect Harbor": In what ways was Puerto Rico a perfect harbor? What did the Spanish have in mind when they said this?

"Three Forts": Why were forts necessary?

"The Walled City": What might it be like to live in a walled city? Has anyone ever lived in or visited a walled city?

"Baseball, Anyone?": Do you think experts were surprised to find that the Indians played a form of baseball? Were you surprised?

Important Vocabulary from the Reading

1. Before they begin to read, be sure that students understand the following words: *environment, strategic, fortress, architecture, convent, ballast, investors,* and *commonwealth.*

2. Have students list the Spanish words in the text and their translations.

3. Discuss cities in the United States that have Spanish names, such as *Los Angeles* and *San Francisco.* Have students guess the meanings of these Spanish names.

Activities to Accompany the Reading

Playing Word Games

Have students work in groups to make lists of words from the reading relating to environment, culture, architecture, and sports. Have them compare lists. Then have them see how many synonyms they can think of for the words on their lists.

Improvising Scenes

1. Have students act out a scene in which Spanish settlers convince leaders that what became San Juan would make a better living site than the old one south of San Juan Bay.

2. Have one student role-play being a tour guide for a visit to Old San Juan.

3. Have students act out a debate on whether remaining a self-governed commonwealth, statehood, or independence is best for Puerto Rico. It might be helpful to provide background information about the November 1993, plebiscite, in which a majority of Puerto Ricans rejected the proposal for statehood.

4. Have a student act as a reporter interviewing Roberto Clemente about his career and Puerto Rican baseball.

BOOK 2

Using Maps

1. On a world map, have students locate the island of Puerto Rico. Also have them find Florida and Spain. Have them find the Atlantic Ocean and the Caribbean Sea.

2. On a topographical map of Puerto Rico, have students find the mountain ranges and the rain forests of Puerto Rico.

Studying Word Parts to Build Vocabulary

Have students notice the -tion suffix, meaning "action or process" in such words as protection, location, and revolution.

Discussion, Writing, or Research Topics

Have students select one of the following topics, do library research on it, and then work with classmates to prepare a group presentation for the class.

- Christopher Columbus's second voyage
- Juan Ponce de León
- Old San Juan
- La Forteleza
- El Morro
- The Spanish-American War
- Indian tribes in Puerto Rico
- Roberto Clemente
- Puerto Rican music, dance, or art
- Games of early Caribbean settlers

Extension Activities

1. Since 1992 was the 500th anniversary of Columbus's arrival in the New World, there are many films and videos available on the subject. Puerto Rican culture is the subject of West Side Story. With its satirical song, "America," as well as its compelling story, the film focuses on Puerto Ricans living in New York City. One of its stars, Rita Moreno, is Puerto Rican. Film stars José Ferrer and Raul Julia are also Puerto Rican. The former may be seen in The Caine Mutiny; the latter, in Kiss of the Spider Woman. Have students see these movies.

2. Have students take a trip to a Puerto Rican restaurant or bakery.

3. Students may visit a museum featuring displays about life in the Caribbean.

For ESL Students

1. If any of the ESL students are Spanish language speakers, have them explain the Spanish words in the story.

2. Have ESL students describe government buildings in their native countries.

3. To practice modals, have students answer the following questions:

- What should you see in Old San Juan?
- How would you have voted in the Puerto Rican election?
- What sports would you like to try in Puerto Rico?
- Could you see a rain forest in Puerto Rico?
- Could you visit underground caves?
- Could you buy refreshments in the plaza?
- Could you buy native handicrafts in the plazas?
- What two languages could you speak in Puerto Rico?
- Where can you find Puerto Rico on a map?

VOCABULARY PRACTICE

A. Use some of these words to complete the sentences that follow.

ballast	mansion	possession
climate	musicians	sculptures
handicrafts	narrow	tunnels
invaders		

1. The _____ at Juan Ponce de León's first location was damp and rainy.

2. _____ from South America, the Carib attacked the fort.

3. After the bigger fort was built, La Forteleza became the governor's

   _____.

4. Puerto Rico became a U.S. _____.

5. _____ in the plaza celebrate Puerto Rican culture and history.

6. One of the forts has mazes of _____ and _____ moats
   filled with water.

B. Use some of these compound words to complete the sentences that follow.

earthquake	lampposts	staircase
headland	northwest	storeroom
horseback	sandstone	sundown

1. The walls to Old San Juan were made of _____.

2. At _____, the gates to Old San Juan were closed.

3. The large fort, El Morro, was built on the _____.

4. There are 20-foot thick walls, a barracks, a dungeon, and a _____
   in the fort.

5. Roberto Clemente died helping _____ victims.

6. _____ riding is popular on the island.

BOOK 2

VOCABULARY PRACTICE (CONTINUED)

C. **In a dictionary, look up the meanings of these words. Then write the definition for each word.**

a mansion and a residence: _____

_____

a harbor and a bay: _____

_____

a cathedral and a chapel: _____

_____

territory, possession, and commonwealth: _____

_____

_____

a journalist and a poet: _____

_____

D. **Use any six words from Part A of this exercise in your own sentences below.**

1. _____

2. _____

3. _____

4. _____

5. _____

6. _____

ATTRACTIONS *Teacher's Guide*
© 1994 Contemporary Books
A Reproducible Exercise Page

READING COMPREHENSION

A. Mark each of these statements *True* or *False*.

_____ **1.** Juan Ponce de Leon first chose to live in San Juan.

_____ **2.** The city gates of Old San Juan are still closed at night.

_____ **3.** The three San Juan forts were all built at the same time.

_____ **4.** The Indian baseball field is the only ceremonial site on the island.

_____ **5.** Two million tourists visit Puerto Rico every year.

_____ **6.** Puerto Rico is not a state.

_____ **7.** There are mountains on the island.

B. What does each word mean in the paragraph indicated? Reread the paragraphs, and circle the letter of the correct answer.

1. gold (3): (a) a yellowish color (b) a precious metal

2. fallen (7): (a) landed in enemy hands (b) been knocked down

3. inhabitants (12): (a) invaders (b) people who live in a place

4. convent (14): (a) a hotel (b) a place where nuns live

5. competitive (20): (a) at a high level of performance (b) casually done

6. resist (22): (a) deny (b) fight off

7. charm (22): (a) lucky item or token (b) attractiveness

BOOK 2

HOMONYMS AND ANTONYMS

A. These pairs are homonyms. (They sound the same.)

gate / gait   weight / wait   right / rite

Say the homonyms above aloud, and then use them to complete these sentences.

1. The _____ to the city was locked at night.

2. Because of his foot injury, his _____ is unnatural.

3. The _____ of the bricks created ballast for the ships from Spain.

4. The governor could not _____ to move into La Forteleza.

5. Was it _____ for Juan Ponce de León to take the gold?

6. What _____ was performed on the ceremonial field?

B. These words are antonyms. (They are opposites.)

agree / disagree   mansion / shack
tourists / inhabitants   solid / liquid

Say the antonyms above aloud. Then use them to complete these sentences.

1. Tourists _____ that Puerto Rico is beautiful.

2. He and his mother _____. She wants to see El Morro. He wants to swim in the ocean.

3. Many _____ visit the island each year.

4. The _____ make money from tourism.

5. The huge stone wall is made of _____ brick.

6. After a day in the sun, I need a refreshing _____.

7. The governor's _____ is like a palace.

8. He lives in a small, unheated _____.

ATTRACTIONS *Teacher's Guide*
© 1994 Contemporary Books
A Reproducible Exercise Page

PARTS OF SPEECH AND INFLECTED FORMS

A. Write the adjective form of each of these nouns:

beauty _____   strategy _____

fertility _____   passion _____

B. Read the adjective forms of the words above aloud. Then use them to complete these sentences.

1. The fort was built at a _____ location.

2. Natives of Puerto Rico are _____ about politics.

3. The _____ harbor at San Juan is very old.

4. _____ land is needed for farming.

WORD PARTS

Study the meaning of these word parts from the reading. Then use them to complete the words in the sentences that follow.

co- = joint, together
de- = away from
-ness and *-ship* = quality or condition of being
sur- = above or over, beyond

1. The relation_____ between Spain and Puerto Rico changed over the years.

2. Forts were built to _____fend San Juan Harbor.

3. Damp_____ was a problem for settlers.

4. The British _____prised the Spanish with their land attack.

5. For the vacation to succeed, the people on the tour must _____operate with their guide.

BOOK 2

PHRASAL VERBS AND OTHER IDIOMS

Reread the paragraphs that the idioms in the column on the left are used in. Then match each idiom with its definition in the column on the right. Write the correct letters on the blank lines.

_____ **1.** impressed by (9)   **(a)** completely occupied by

_____ **2.** filled with (14)   **(b)** affected positively

_____ **3.** on foot (15)   **(c)** located on

_____ **4.** to be found on (19)   **(d)** professional sports organization

_____ **5.** major leagues (20)   **(e)** walking

PATTERN PRACTICE

Use an appropriate verb to complete each sentence. The verb should be in past-tense and passive-voice form. For the information you need, reread the paragraphs indicated.

1. La Forteleza _____ not originally _____ to be a governor's mansion. (8)

2. The problem of muddy streets _____ by blue bricks imported from Spain. (15)

3. Scientists think that baseball _____ by Indians in a ceremonial park. (18)

4. These ceremonial parks _____ by scientists. (19)

5. Baseball _____ by many famous Puerto Ricans. (20)

6. Last year, other sports _____ by tourists and natives alike. (21)

ATTRACTIONS *Teacher's Guide*
© 1994 Contemporary Books
A Reproducible Exercise Page

NEON OASIS

(PAGES 3–13)

Pre-Reading Activities

Discussion Questions

1. About Las Vegas: Where is it? Why is it such a popular tourist spot? Why is it sometimes called Lost Wages? What's the climate like there?

2. About the psychology of gambling: Why do people gamble? Do they really want to win, or do they want to lose? Is it so popular because, in games of luck, everyone is equal?

3. About gambling opportunities: What kinds of legalized gambling are available outside Nevada? What kinds of gambling are allowed in the state you live in? What kinds of gambling are illegal in most places? What new forms of gambling have become available in your part of the country? Why have more and more states been encouraging gambling in recent years?

4. About Nevada: What is the state famous for besides gambling?

5. About Hoover Dam: Why is a dam usually built? What benefits does it bring to an area? Why is Hoover Dam especially impressive?

6. About the title: Why is Las Vegas called a neon oasis?

7. About the photographs accompanying this reading: Who's shown in the full-page photo? (He's Vegas Vic, the neon cowboy.)

8. About the teaser: How many tourists do you think Las Vegas attracts each year? (Paragraph 4 answers the question. Students may also look for the reasons for Las Vegas's great popularity with tourists.)

Section Headings

"A High-Stakes Gamble": Have students define a *high-stakes gamble*. The general meaning is a bet of a large sum or great risk. Have them read the first paragraph to find out who took a high-stakes gamble and what he risked. Ask them if his gamble paid off.

"City of Lights": Ask students what kind of signs Las Vegas is famous for. Have them read paragraph 6 to find out. Then discuss what neon lights are and what makes signs lit with them so bright and appealing.

"The Strip": Ask students what the Strip is.

"The Odds Aren't With You": Discuss the meaning of odds in betting. Ask students why the odds aren't with the bettor in Las Vegas.

"Las Vegas—Then and Now": Point out that this title prepares the reader for a chronological account that involves comparison and contrast.

Important Vocabulary from the Reading

1. Before students begin the chapter, briefly explain some of the common gambling games, or at least tell which are card games, dice games, and wheel games. Mention poker, craps, roulette, blackjack, bingo, keno, and Wheel of Fortune. Also, explain slot machines and video slot machines.

2. Define the following gambling vocabulary: *high stakes, high roller, odds, even money,* and *house advantage.*

3. Discuss these geological words from the reading. They include *canyon, oasis, spring, glacial lake,* and *desert.*

4. Discuss the following homonyms and similar words:

   • *miner* and *minor*: Note that *minors* are usually people under the age of 18. But in terms of gambling and buying alcohol, in some places people must be 21 years old to be allowed to gamble or buy alcohol. *Miners* are mentioned in the chapter because they worked on the Hoover Dam.

   • *better* and *bettor*: The first is a comparative form; the second is a person placing a bet.

   • *recreation* and *re-creation*: The first is leisure-time activity; the second is a copy. The first word has a short vowel sound; the second, a long one.

   • *big-shot*, adjective and *big shot*, noun: Note that the adjective is hyphenated. But the words are not hyphenated if *shot* is being used as a noun. Compare these sentences: "He's a *big-shot* gambler" and "He thinks he's a *big shot.*"

Activities to Accompany the Reading

Playing Word Games

1. Play this word game. The object of the game is to think of as many meanings of the word *shot* as possible. It may be played competitively with teams of two or three and a time limit. To get students started, point out the two uses found in paragraph 1 of the reading. Figurative and slang expressions are acceptable. Answers will include an injection, a golfer's shot, a shot of whiskey, and "take a shot," which means *try*.

2. Play this word game. This reading contains two words with the suffix *-ize*, *legalized* and *publicized*. They are past participles used as adjectives. Remind students that *-ize* is a verb ending. It means "to cause to be," "to become," or "to make something resemble." The object of this timed game is to list as many words ending with *-ize* as possible. They must be spelled correctly to count. Here are some answers to expect: *memorize, dramatize, sterilize, customize, deodorize, sanitize, democratize, revolutionize, authorize,* and *recognize*.

Improvising Scenes

Have one student act as the Las Vegas casino "teacher," explaining how to play a particular game to the Las Vegas visitors (the other students in the class). The "teacher" should have some visual aids—cards, dice, or a photocopy of a craps layout. Several students may play "teacher," each explaining a different game.

Comparing and Contrasting

Have students reread the section headed "Las Vegas—Then and Now." Then have them contrast the city of 1935 with the city of today.

Using Maps

On a map of the United States, find Nevada, Las Vegas, the Hoover Dam, Lake Mead, and Lake Tahoe. Point out why people going from Santa Fe, New Mexico, to California might stop at Las Vegas.

Discussion, Writing, or Research Topics

1. Have students tell about a time when they bet on something. Then have them write about the experience.

2. Have two teams of four students debate this statement: "All forms of gambling should be legalized in all states." The other students, the audience, might then write a paragraph telling which side they think won the debate.

3. Gambling is a very ancient form of recreation that seems to have been practiced in some form all over the world throughout history. Have students read about gambling in other times and places and write a paragraph summarizing the most interesting kind of gambling they read about. Offer a prize, perhaps a lottery ticket, to the researcher who finds the most interesting game.

Extension Activities

1. Have students do some library and/or telephone research to find out what kinds of gambling are legal in their state.

2. One class period could be Casino Day, during which students play a few of the common casino games using fake money.

3. Have a local speaker talk to the class about treatment for compulsive gamblers or about illegal gambling activities to avoid.

For ESL Students

1. Have students discuss the attitude toward gambling in their country, ethnic group, or religion.

2. Make a list of expressions that include the word *high*. Some are in the reading (*high roller* and *high-stakes*). Some others to teach include *high* (meaning "drunk"), *highbrow, high and dry, highway robbery,* and *high-tech* (technology).

3. Make a list of expressions that include the word *big*. (The reading includes *big shot* and *big-name*. Some others are *big deal, big time, big business, bighearted*.

READING COMPREHENSION

A. Mark each of these statements *True* or *False*.

_____ **1.** More visitors come to Las Vegas than to Orlando, Florida, the home of Walt Disney World.

_____ **2.** Gambling is the only Las Vegas attraction.

_____ **3.** Because Las Vegas is so hot, the city's population is decreasing.

_____ **4.** In Las Vegas, the chances of winning money in a gambling casino are about the same no matter which game you play.

_____ **5.** It's easy to get married or divorced anywhere in Nevada.

B. Reread each paragraph indicated. Then write a question you can answer with information from that paragraph. Then answer each question with a complete sentence.

1. Paragraph 8:

Question: _____

Answer: _____

2. Paragraph 15:

Question: _____

Answer: _____

3. Paragraph 21:

Question: _____

Answer: _____

4. Paragraph 26:

Question: _____

Answer: _____

5. Paragraph 28:

Question: _____

Answer: _____

BOOK 3

READING COMPREHENSION (CONTINUED)

C. Circle the letter of the best answer to complete each sentence.

1. According to paragraphs 8 and 9, summers in Las Vegas are (a) hot and humid (b) hot and dry (c) windy and rainy.

2. The main idea of paragraph 17 is stated in (a) the first sentence (b) the second sentence (c) the last sentence.

3. According to paragraph 20, Las Vegas was a real oasis because it had (a) a lot of caravans stopping there (b) water (c) the Old Spanish Trail.

4. According to paragraphs 21–23, Hoover Dam was built (a) to create a big lake (b) to be a source of water and electric power (c) to get rock from a canyon.

5. According to paragraph 26, the main reason that so many people get married in Nevada is because (a) there's a residency requirement (b) there are a lot of wedding chapels (c) they can get married quickly.

D. Scan the reading and the Sidelights page to find the following information.

1. the number of tourists that visit Las Vegas annually: _____

2. the average annual rainfall in Las Vegas: _____ in Nevada: _____

3. the cost of the most expensive hotel ever built in Las Vegas: _____

4. the amount of money that Las Vegas casinos take in daily: _____

5. the year the first Las Vegas luxury hotel opened: _____

6. the height of Hoover Dam: _____

7. the number of marriages performed annually in Las Vegas: _____

8. Nevada's residency requirement for obtaining a divorce: _____

NAME _____

VOCABULARY PRACTICE

A. Use some of these phrases to complete the sentences that follow.

> annual rainfall   over budget   regular customer
> high-stakes   parental consent   residency requirement
> minimum age   real estate   widely publicized

1. She sells buildings and land. She sells _____.

2. I buy most of my groceries at this supermarket. I'm a _____ there.

3. You need to register to vote. But first, you must live in this town for three months. That's the _____.

4. My vacation in Las Vegas cost me twice as much as I had expected. I went _____.

5. In most states, a 16-year-old cannot get married without _____.

B. Circle the word that best completes each sentence.

1. Las Vegas hotels have fancy gambling (debts, malls, odds, casinos).

2. Las Vegas has a lot of colorful signs, so it's called a (retirement, neon, periodic, skimpy) oasis.

3. A desert climate has a low (temperature, dusk, dome, humidity).

4. A wheel is needed to play (roulette, craps, neon, keno).

5. A manmade lake is a (bay, spring, oasis, reservoir).

6. Gambling and fancy hotels attract people to Las Vegas. In other words, the hotels and casinos (shift, lure, erupt, allow) them there.

7. An oasis is found in a (reservoir, dam, desert, forest).

8. A volcano sometimes (overflows, erupts, floods, booms).

BOOK 3

WORDS IN CONTEXT

What do the underlined phrases mean in this reading? Reread the paragraphs indicated. Then circle the letter of the correct answer.

1. In paragraph 1, <u>a big-shot gangster</u> means (a) a lot of people shot at him (b) he was considered important and influential.

2. In paragraph 2, <u>curious people</u> means (a) people who were interested in learning more about something (b) people who were very strange and interesting.

3. In paragraph 4, <u>head straight for</u> means (a) travel on a straight road (b) go to a place without stopping somewhere else first.

4. In paragraph 8, <u>rarely does it rain</u> means (a) it rains a lot (b) it almost never rains.

5. In paragraph 8, <u>humidity</u> means (a) the temperature (b) the amount of moisture in the air.

6. In paragraph 11, <u>bay</u> means (a) a small body of water (b) a small piece of land.

7. In paragraph 21, <u>the Depression</u> means (a) a continuing feeling of sadness (b) a period of large-scale unemployment.

8. In paragraph 24, <u>springing up</u> means (a) being constructed rapidly (b) jumping high in the air.

HOMONYMS, SYNONYMS, AND SIMILAR WORDS

Match each word in the column on the left with the correct word or phrase in the column on the right. Write the correct letters on the blank lines.

_____ 1. construct   **(a)** customers

_____ 2. gamble   **(b)** bet

_____ 3. lavish   **(c)** attract

_____ 4. lure   **(d)** occurring from time to time

_____ 5. patrons   **(e)** extravagant

_____ 6. periodic   **(f)** build

ATTRACTIONS *Teacher's Guide*
© 1994 Contemporary Books
A Reproducible Exercise Page

PATTERN PRACTICE

Reread paragraph 17. Notice the sentences that begin with *if*. Now complete the sentences below using information from the reading. You can complete the sentences in a variety of ways.

Examples: If you like to gamble, <u>take</u> a vacation in Las Vegas. (imperative form)

If you like to gamble, you <u>should go</u> to Las Vegas. (present modal)

If you like to gamble, you <u>will enjoy</u> a vacation in Las Vegas. (future)

1. If you enjoy swimming and boating, _____.

2. If you're 21 years old or older, _____.

3. If you go to Las Vegas, _____.

4. _____ if you go to the Strip.

PARTS OF SPEECH AND INFLECTED FORMS

A. Some of these words are always adjectives. Some are usually nouns. Put a check (✓) after the ones that are usually nouns.

concrete	gambling	parental
curious	glass	pirate
erupting	health	wedding

B. All of the words above can be used as adjectives to describe a noun. Use some of them to complete these phrases.

Example: a health spa

1. a _____ casino

2. a _____ ceremony

3. a _____ dam

4. a _____ dome

5. _____ consent

6. _____ people

7. a _____ ship

8. an _____ volcano

BOOK 3

WORD PARTS

Study these word parts from the reading.

> con-, com- = with, together
> de- = down, away from
> extra- = outside, beyond, more than
>
> re- + serv = to store, keep or hold back
> re- + venue = to return, come back

Use the correct word parts above to complete the words in these sentences.

1. The water stopped by the Hoover Dam is stored in a _____oir.

2. To stay in a luxury hotel in Las Vegas, you need to make a _____ation.

3. The words _____bine, _____nect, and _____vention are about bringing people or things together.

4. The shows in Las Vegas are _____vagant. They're very lavish.

5. The downturn in the economy indicates a coming _____pression.

6. In Las Vegas, the money that casinos earn is called _____.

PHRASAL VERBS AND OTHER IDIOMS

Reread the paragraphs these phrases are used in. The paragraph numbers are in parentheses. Then use some of the phrases to complete the sentences that follow.

> big shot (1)
> high roller (2)
> a piece of the action (2)
>
> big-name (12)
> chorus line (12)
> in the long run (15)
>
> no-frills (26)
> boom (28)
> no longer (28)

1. George quit his job. He is _____ employed here.

2. The show featured a _____ of 20 dancers.

3. If you gamble regularly, it will cost you money _____.

4. He wants to get into that poker game. He wants _____.

5. He's a very important person. He's a _____.

ATTRACTIONS *Teacher's Guide*
© 1994 Contemporary Books
A Reproducible Exercise Page

ELVIS'S KINGDOM

(PAGES 17–29)

Pre-Reading Activities

Discussion Questions

1. About Elvis Presley: Why was he famous? Do you like his music and performance style? Why? When was he born? Which years was he most popular? When did he die? How old was he at the time of his death?

2. About the Elvis myth: What unusual things have happened to his image and career since he died?

3. About Graceland: Where is Elvis's home? Have you ever visited it? Do you know anything about what's in it? Why is the home's name appropriate for Elvis's house? (Elvis was very religious, so the name fits. However, he didn't name it Graceland. The preceding owner gave it that name, after her aunt.)

4. About Memphis: Besides being Elvis's home, what else is the city famous for? What state and section of the country is it in? Why is it important in American musical history? (Sidelights provides some answers.)

5. About Tennessee: What is the other major city in Tennessee? Why is it important in American musical history? (Nashville is the country music capital of the United States.)

6. About the photographs: Does the exterior of Elvis's home fit his image? Why or why not? What about the gate?

7. About the title of the reading: In what ways was Elvis a king with a kingdom? In what ways was he a prisoner in a luxurious prison?

8. About the teaser: How many hit singles do you think Elvis had? (Paragraph 26 answers the question.)

Section Headings

"Long Live the King!": Ask students if there has been a rock 'n' roll successor to Elvis, the King. Also, point out that Elvis's memory has been kept alive.

"From Rags to Riches": Discuss the meaning of this saying. Compare it with calling Elvis "a self-made man," in paragraph 22. Discuss the fact that Americans particularly admire someone who "makes it" on his or her own. Ask them to name other famous Americans who have done that.

"Movies and Marriage": Point out that this heading suggests some connection between movies and marriage in Elvis's life. Remind students to look for that connection when they read the section.

"A Downhill Slide": Point out that this saying is usually "sliding downhill." Discuss what kinds of behavior make a person slide downhill. Ask students which of them were significant in Elvis's life.

"Visiting Graceland": As the title indicates, this section presents information from the tourists' point of view.

"The Stamp of Success": Discuss both the literal and the figurative meanings of this subhead (the postage stamp and the honor that it conveyed). Ask students if they like the younger Elvis better and why they think young Elvis won.

Important Vocabulary from the Reading

1. Discuss these types of music: gospel, blues, country music, and western music. Discuss the meaning of chords and a musical beat.

2. Discuss the following vocabulary relating to money: *million, billion, financial, royalties, estate,* and *earnings.* Be sure that students know how many thousands make a million and how many millions make a billion.

3. Define these words about cooking: *recipe* and *ingredient.*

4. Define this clothing: *jumpsuit, gold lamé jacket.*

5. Distinguish between these types of drugs: prescription and over-the-counter; legal and illegal.

Activities to Accompany the Reading

Playing Word Games

Have students work in pairs to list as many adjectives as they can to describe Elvis. Allow three minutes. Students may not use the text. Each adjective counts as 1 point, with 1/2 point off if it's misspelled.

Improvising Scenes

1. Watch a few scenes from an Elvis Presley movie. Then cast students in various roles. After watching the scene a second time, students should re-create it, paraphrasing and ad-libbing their dialogue.

2. Are there any Elvis impersonators in the class? Have them lip-sync some songs.

Comparing and Contrasting

1. Discuss Elvis's strengths and weaknesses as described in this reading.

2. Compare and contrast his childhood and his adulthood.

Using Maps

On a U.S. map, find the places mentioned in the reading: Mississippi, Tennessee, California, and Las Vegas, Nevada. They are all places where Elvis lived and worked.

Discussion, Writing, or Research Topics

1. Ask students the following questions about their reaction to the reading:

   - Did it make you admire Elvis more or less than before?
   - What information in the reading surprised you?
   - Did the reading make you want to visit Graceland?
   - After completing the reading, did you feel that Elvis accomplished anything important in his life?
   - If Elvis hadn't died when he did, what do you think would have happened to his personal life and his career?

2. Have students write a paragraph about what Elvis's biggest mistake was.

3. Compare the sayings "Gone but not forgotten" and "Out of sight, out of mind." Ask students which one they think is usually true and why.

Extension Activities

1. Have students get a videotape of an Elvis movie, watch it at home, and then write a movie review. Give them specific questions to answer, such as

   - Was the story believable?
   - Was Elvis's acting good?
   - Did the language seem old-fashioned?
   - Did the moral values seem old-fashioned?
   - Did you like the movie?

2. Have students listen to some Elvis songs at home and write down the lyrics to their favorites. Then have them bring the tapes to school. Pass out copies of the lyrics and have a sing-along. Then discuss the meanings of the songs.

3. Listen with the class to some of today's rock 'n' roll songs. Ask students whether the words and music are much different than those of Elvis's time.

For ESL Students

1. Ask students for different meanings of *grave*, *hit*, *fan*, and *moonlight*.

2. Point out the difference in pronunciation between *live* as an adjective, as in a *live* audience, and *live* as a verb, as in I *live* in Maine. Also, compare these words to *alive*.

3. Have students list the names of the rooms in the typical American home. Some of them are in the reading. Pronounce *bathroom* and *bedroom*.

4. Ask students if they had heard of Elvis before this reading. Take a vote. Discuss what the results show about his continuing fame.

READING COMPREHENSION

A. Mark each of these statements *True* or *False*.

_____ **1.** Elvis was a rebel who refused to obey authority.

_____ **2.** Elvis spent, lost, or gave away most of the money he earned.

_____ **3.** Elvis could play the piano better than the guitar.

_____ **4.** Elvis's fans called him the King because he was very rich.

_____ **5.** Elvis is a good example of the expression "gone but not forgotten."

B. Answer these questions about the reading in complete sentences.

1. Why did Elvis become such a famous performer?

_____

2. In what ways did Elvis slide downhill in the last years of his life?

_____

3. Is Graceland a more popular tourist site than the White House?

_____

4. What can visitors see inside Graceland?

_____

5. What two dates in Elvis's life are most important to his fans? Why is each one important?

_____

_____

6. Would you like to live the way Elvis did? _____
Why or why not? _____

_____

BOOK 3

READING COMPREHENSION (CONTINUED)

C. Scan the paragraphs indicated to find the answers to these questions.

What pieces of information show that Elvis has not been forgotten? (1–6) Write three sentences about ways in which he's remembered.

1. _____

2. _____

3. _____

What styles of music did Elvis combine in rockabilly? (8)

4. _____

Name four of Elvis's good qualities. (32)

5. _____ _____ _____ _____

D. Reread the paragraphs indicated. Then make inferences to answer the following questions. Support your inferences by writing the clues provided in the paragraph.

1. Did Elvis have a loving mother? (8) _____
   What information suggests that?

   _____

   _____

2. Did Elvis love his mother? (9) _____
   What information suggests that?

   _____

   _____

3. What does the Elvis quotation in paragraph 20 suggest?

   _____

   _____

ATTRACTIONS *Teacher's Guide*
© 1994 Contemporary Books
A Reproducible Exercise Page

VOCABULARY PRACTICE

Read these words aloud, and discuss their meanings. Then use some of them to complete the sentences that follow.

anniversary	fans	impersonate	royalties
decorated	fuss	ingredients	scripts
display	gospel	notice	souvenirs
entertain	grave	recipes	victim

1. A birthday is the _____ of a person's birth.

2. Elvis Presley's _____ made a lot of fuss over him.

3. Thousands of people come to Elvis's _____ on his death date.

4. Elvis _____ his home in bright colors and fancy furniture.

5. At the Graceland Plaza, many people buy _____.

6. In church, Elvis heard _____ singing.

7. Elvis Presley's awards, clothing, and airplanes are on _____ at Graceland and at the nearby mall.

8. Some of the Presley family's favorite _____ are in a cookbook that tourists can buy. Each recipe lists the _____.

9. Some people who look and dress like Elvis _____ him onstage and make a good living.

10. Some of Elvis's earnings came from _____ on the songs he recorded.

11. Some people think that Elvis was a _____ of fame and great wealth.

12. Performers are people who _____ the public.

BOOK 3

WORDS IN CONTEXT

What does each underlined phrase mean in this reading? Reread each paragraph. Then circle the letter of the correct answer.

1. In paragraph 3, <u>it's priceless</u> means (a) no one has offered to buy it (b) it's too valuable to even imagine the price.

2. In paragraph 10, <u>limited skills on the guitar</u> means (a) he was a very good guitarist (b) he could play the guitar a little.

3. In paragraph 13, <u>financial success</u> means (a) making money (b) succeeding after a long time.

4. In paragraph 24, <u>lavish taste</u> means (a) good food (b) a love of fancy things.

5. In paragraph 33, <u>won by a landslide</u> means (a) won a race by going very fast (b) won by a large number of votes.

HOMONYMS, SYNONYMS, AND SIMILAR WORDS

Match each word in the column on the left with the correct word or phrase in the column on the right. Write the correct letters on the blank lines.

_____ 1. devotion   **(a)** see, observe

_____ 2. career   **(b)** show publicly

_____ 3. concert   **(c)** admirer

_____ 4. display   **(d)** musical performance

_____ 5. fan   **(e)** profession, occupation, work

_____ 6. notice   **(f)** dedication

ATTRACTIONS *Teacher's Guide*
© 1994 Contemporary Books
A Reproducible Exercise Page

PATTERN PRACTICE

In the first sentence in paragraph 31, two contrasting ideas are connected with *although*. Connect the ideas in these sentences. Use *although* instead of *but*.

1. Elvis was a very poor child, but he was a very rich adult.

Although _____.

2. Elvis's movies were popular with fans, but Elvis didn't like them very much.

Although _____.

3. Elvis performed with an electric guitar, but he played the piano much better.

_____, although

_____.

PARTS OF SPEECH AND INFLECTED FORMS

Use words from these verb-noun pairs to complete the sentences that follow. Put the verbs in the correct tense.

appear / appearance	decorate / decoration	respond / response
bury / burial	die / death	succeed / success
combine / combination	marry / marriage	weigh / weight

1. Elvis Presley was 42 years old at the time of his _____.

2. Did he _____ in living a happy life?

3. Elvis ate too much and gained a lot of _____.

4. Perhaps he had a heart attack because he _____ so much.

5. Meditation Garden is the Presley family's _____ site.

6. Elvis's style _____ several types of music.

7. Was Elvis's life a _____ or a failure?

8. Do you think Elvis wanted to _____ because he wasn't happy with his life?

BOOK 3

WORD PARTS

Some nouns can be made into adjectives by adding the ending *-ful*, meaning "full of," or *-less*, meaning "without." Use some of these adjectives to complete the sentences that follow.

awful	careless	priceless	tearful
careful	harmless	successful	wonderful

1. When you drive a car, you should be _____.

2. Something that is not dangerous is _____.

3. Elvis Presley's fans thought he was _____, but the people at Grand Ole Opry thought he was _____.

4. Every day, _____ fans come to put flowers on Elvis's grave.

5. A _____ possession is very valuable.

PHRASAL VERBS AND OTHER IDIOMS

Reread the paragraphs that these idioms are used in. The paragraph numbers are in parentheses. Then use the idioms to complete the sentences that follow.

downhill slide (subhead above 18) = get worse
flop (9) = a failure
hit (26) = very popular
settle down (16) = get married, calm down
took off (10) = improved

1. When a record is a _____, it sells well.

2. When people don't like a performer, he or she is a _____.

3. Elvis's career _____ when he was a young man.

4. Please be quiet. _____.

5. Elvis's career took a _____ in the mid-1970s.

ATTRACTIONS *Teacher's Guide*
© 1994 Contemporary Books
A Reproducible Exercise Page

ENCHANTED LAND

(PAGES 33–43)

Pre-Reading Activities

Discussion Questions

1. About New Mexico: What comes to mind about this state? Can you name any of its cities? What ethnic groups live in New Mexico? What is the state's connection to nuclear power? What are its climate and geography like?

2. About Native Americans: What states do you think have the largest Native American populations? Why? What are some of the tragic experiences that Native Americans have had to endure since Europeans came to the Western Hemisphere?

3. About Georgia O'Keeffe: Who was she? How old was she when she died? (almost 100) Have you ever seen any of her work? (Show some to the class, especially her paintings of New Mexico.)

4. About Kit Carson: Is the name familiar to you? Was he a "good guy" or a "bad guy"? (Give students some background about this Indian fighter who liked and was liked by the Indians he had to relocate.)

5. About the chapter title: What does *enchant* mean? (It comes from French and Latin. It originally meant "to bewitch or cast a spell over." Today, its more common English meaning is "to delight, charm, fascinate, or captivate.") Have you ever been to a place that enchanted you? Where was it? What did you like about it? Do you plan to go back? Do you want to live there?

6. About the photographs accompanying the reading: What do they reveal about New Mexico's geography? Its population? Do the illustrations make you want to visit New Mexico? What interests you most?

7. About the teaser: What's the most photographed sporting event in the world? (The answer is hot-air ballooning, shown in the photograph on page 32 and on the cover of the book. See paragraph 18 for information about this sport. Because these colorful balloons look so beautiful in the air, they are very popular as photographic subjects.)

Section Headings

"Wild Places, Open Spaces": Explain to students that *wild* here refers to wilderness, to undeveloped areas. Much of New Mexico is desert. It isn't sand, but it is dry land with low shrubbery. These are open spaces because the areas are flat and uninhabited by people.

"A Salad Bowl": Discuss the differences between a salad bowl and a melting pot as metaphors for multicultural communities.

"A Long History": Ask students what this expression means. It means that the history goes far back in time. In the case of New Mexico, human habitation goes back at least to 20,000 B.C.

"Going Up": This section is about Albuquerque. It focuses on two exciting rides that tourists take there: a tram ride and a hot-air balloon ride.

"Santa Fe": Ask students what they expect to find out about this city in this section. The book's emphasis is on popular tourist attractions, so the section focuses on what tourists can see and do there.

"Taos": Have students read this short section (paragraphs 25 and 26) to find out why tourists go to this small town.

Important Vocabulary from the Reading

1. Define the following Spanish words:

   bonito = pretty or cute
   piñon = pine nut seed
   fiesta = party or holiday
   El Camino Real = the Royal Road
   pueblo = village

2. Discuss the following Spanish words:

   - *adobe*: In Spanish, the word means "dried brick." It refers to sun-dried clay bricks and the style of dwellings common in New Mexico, southern California, and Mexico that are built with these bricks.
   - *chili*: The Spanish word *chili* (or *chile*) means "red pepper." The word refers to the dried pod of red pepper and to the tropical American plant that bears this pod. There are many varieties of chilis. (The plural is also spelled *chiles*.) Chili is also a Mexican dish made of minced red peppers and kidney beans. When it has meat in it, it's called *chili con carne.*

- *rodeo*: Contrast the Spanish pronunciation, [row•day'oh], and the American pronunciation, [row'dee•oh]. To Americans and Mexicans, the word now means an exhibition or competition of the skills of cowboys with horses and cattle. In its older Spanish meaning, a *rodeo* was an enclosed space for cattle that had been rounded up for sale or branding.
- Santa Fe: The name means holy faith.

3. Review the differences in spelling and pronunciation between a *dessert*, a *desert*, and to *desert*.

Activities to Accompany the Reading

Playing Word Games

Have students work individually and scan the reading to complete a list of names of Native American groups and a list of famous people from the text. Set a brief time limit on this game. Give one point for each correct name.

Improvising Scenes

Separate the class into groups. In each group, one or two people act as the tourists and another person acts as the travel agent. The travel agent answers questions about New Mexico and helps the tourists plan their trip there.

Using Maps

1. On a U.S. map, find New Mexico, Albuquerque, Santa Fe, and Taos.

2. The Santa Fe Trail was one of the country's longest trade routes in the period before railroads. This route went from Independence, Missouri, to Santa Fe, a distance of 780 miles. Find a description of the route in any encyclopedia, and have students trace it on a map.

3. The Old Spanish Trail was an extension of the Santa Fe Trail. It ran from Santa Fe to Los Angeles in a semicircular route by way of Durango, Colorado, the Green and Virgin Rivers in Utah, the Colorado River, and across the Mojave Desert in California. Have students trace this route.

Discussion, Writing, or Research Topics

1. Review proper business letter form. Have students write a letter to some city or tourist site they would like to visit. Have them ask for information about how to get there and what to see in the area. After they receive the information, have them prepare a brief oral report to tell their classmates about vacationing in the area they wrote to.

2. Have students pretend to be newspaper reporters and interview someone who has visited or lived in New Mexico. Have the group list some good questions to ask. Then have them write up the interview, using a question and answer format.

Extension Activities

1. Have students plan a trip to New Mexico by car, bus, train, or airplane. Have each student research by phone the time and cost of the type of transportation he or she plans to use. Students who want to drive there may get a route from a computer program or a map.

2. Have students form groups and do library research on the following people mentioned in the reading: Georgia O'Keeffe, Robert Goddard, Geronimo, and Kit Carson. Students might rent the 1993 movie *Geronimo*. Have each group tell the rest of the class about the life and accomplishments of each famous person.

For ESL Students

Explain the difference between countable and uncountable nouns. Then have students scan the reading for as many uncountable nouns as they can find. Their list should include the following: *research, equipment, lava, daybreak*, and *scenery*. Other very common uncountable nouns not in the reading are *money, music, water, sugar, sand*, and *luggage*. Students should also realize that many English words are sometimes countable and sometimes uncountable, such as *time, wine*, and *fruit*.

READING COMPREHENSION

A. Mark each of these statements *True* or *False*.

_____ **1.** The main ethnic groups in New Mexico are artists and scientists.

_____ **2.** New Mexico has a lot of land and a rather small population compared to other states.

_____ **3.** The word *pueblo* is the name of a type of community and an Indian group.

_____ **4.** Missionaries are American Indian religious leaders.

_____ **5.** New Mexico is very proud of its history of bloody ethnic battles.

B. Complete these sentences.

1. If Kit Carson returned to New Mexico today, he would be happy because

_____.

2. Artists like Santa Fe because

_____.

3. Many nuclear scientists have chosen to do research in New Mexico because

_____.

4. The nuns of Loretto Chapel couldn't get up to their choir loft because

_____.

5. Cultural diversity makes New Mexico an interesting tourist spot because

_____.

6. In paragraph 17, there are quotation marks around the word *live* because

_____.

7. The Sidelights page says that Carlsbad Caverns is interesting because

_____.

8. Smoky Bear was named "Smoky" because

_____.

BOOK 3

NAME _____

READING COMPREHENSION (CONTINUED)

C. Answer these questions about the reading.

1. In paragraph 7, what word tells you that not all Native Americans live on reservations? _____

2. In paragraph 8, what is unexpected about the ways in which pueblos honor their patron saints? _____

3. According to paragraphs 9 and 10, what New Mexican foods are not a traditional part of the Mexican diet? _____

4. In paragraph 15, what word tells you that the streets in Albuquerque's Old Town aren't straight? _____

5. According to paragraph 16, why do tourists take the tram to the top of the mountain? _____

6. In paragraph 19, what words tell you that hot-air balloons are sometimes noisy?

_____

D. Match each numeral in the column on the left with the correct word or phrase in the column on the right. Write the correct letters on the blank lines.

_____ **1.** 7,000 feet

_____ **2.** 70 miles

_____ **3.** 16 million acres

_____ **4.** the year 1945

_____ **5.** the year 1610

_____ **6.** 20,000 B.C.

_____ **7.** 56,500

_____ **8.** 200,000

(a) earliest human residents of New Mexico

(b) Santa Fe's elevation above sea level

(c) Palace of Governors was built

(d) distance between Santa Fe and Taos

(e) size of the Navaho reservation

(f) world's first atomic explosion

(g) New Mexico's Hispanic population

(h) number of residents in Santa Fe

ATTRACTIONS *Teacher's Guide*
© 1994 Contemporary Books
A Reproducible Exercise Page

VOCABULARY PRACTICE

A. Use these words to fill in the blanks that follow.

acre	diversity	obvious	rodeo
adobe	exceed	pueblo	solar
chili	exhibit	reservation	solution
conducting	fiesta	resort	visibility

1. an _____ house

2. the Navaho _____

3. cultural _____

4. _____ research

5. riding a bull in a _____

6. 4,840 square yards = an _____

7. International Hot-Air Balloon _____

8. the _____ system

B. Circle the word that doesn't belong in each group.

1. <u>a city</u>: Taos, Anasazi, Albuquerque, Pueblo, Las Cruces

2. <u>a New Mexican crop</u>: pottery, nuts, chilis, apples, cotton

3. <u>an occupation</u>: saint, carpenter, explorer, soldier, missionary

4. <u>an Indian group</u>: Anasazi, Geronimo, Pueblo, Apache, Navaho

5. <u>Native American crafts</u>: baskets, jewelry, dances, blankets, pottery

6. <u>a community</u>: colony, pueblo, trapper, province, reservation

C. Circle the word that best completes each sentence.

1. Many types of (corn, cactus, lava, colony) grow in deserts.

2. Robert Goddard was a (missionary, saint, scientist, warrior).

3. *Sopaipilla* is a (desert, dessert, nut, adobe).

4. In Santa Fe, tourists browse in many art (legends, galleries, pueblos, zones).

BOOK 3

WORDS IN CONTEXT

What does each word mean in the paragraph indicated? Reread the paragraphs. Then circle the letter of the correct answer.

1. <u>density</u> (3): (a) the average number of people in each section of an area (b) the total population of a place

2. <u>white-water rafting</u> (20): (a) riding a raft on very clear water (b) riding a raft on fast-flowing water over rapids

3. <u>prehistoric Indians</u> (20): (a) Indians that aren't written about in the history books (b) Indians that lived before the earliest period of recorded history

4. <u>at least</u> (25): (a) about (b) that amount or more

HOMONYMS, SYNONYMS, AND SIMILAR WORDS

Which of these pairs of words mean about the same? Circle them. Which are different? List them and explain the differences on the lines below. Use a dictionary for help, if necessary.

arts / crafts	prehistoric / ancient
breathtaking / outstanding	raw / cooked
diversity / variety	warrior / fighter (in military battles)
fiesta / celebration	winding / spiraling

_____

_____

_____

_____

_____

_____

_____

_____

ATTRACTIONS *Teacher's Guide*
© 1994 Contemporary Books
A Reproducible Exercise Page

PATTERN PRACTICE

Complete each sentence with three words or phrases. Use information from the reading.

Example: The Pueblo Indians grew <u>corn, beans, and squash.</u>

1. Kit Carson was a famous _____

_____.

2. The advanced culture of the Anasazi Indians had _____

_____.

3. In New Mexico, there were bloody battles between _____

_____.

4. Albuquerque's Old Town has _____

_____.

5. New Mexico has _____.

6. American Indians make _____.

7. In New Mexico, there are Hispanic influences in _____

_____.

PARTS OF SPEECH AND INFLECTED FORMS

Write a plural form of these nouns. Some are irregular. Some have two correct forms.

1. bear _____   6. deer _____

2. bison _____   7. gallery _____

3. chili _____   8. life _____

4. cactus _____   9. sheep _____

5. corn _____   10. variety _____

ATTRACTIONS *Teacher's Guide*
© 1994 Contemporary Books
A Reproducible Exercise Page

BOOK 3

WORD PARTS

Use these word parts to complete the words in the sentences that follow.

ex- = away from, beyond, former   *multi-* = many
-glyph = a carved figure   *out-* = away from, better, greater, more than
-less = without   *petro-* = rock or stone

1. Petro_____ National Park has ancient drawings carved into hardened lava.

2. A hot-air balloonist can _____plore the clouds.

3. A _____-story building has many floors.

4. San Diego has _____standing cultural institutions including a fine symphony orchestra.

5. In some places in New Mexico, the desert seems to go on end_____ly.

PHRASAL VERBS AND OTHER IDIOMS

Reread the paragraphs that the underlined expressions are used in. The paragraph numbers are in parentheses. Then answer the questions.

1. How do you feel when something is <u>too close for comfort</u>? (2) _____

   _____

2. Why was the United States called a <u>melting pot</u>? (5) _____

   _____

3. Where is <u>open-air</u> opera performed? (21) _____

4. What makes New Mexico a <u>land of enchantment</u>? (27) _____

   _____

ATTRACTIONS *Teacher's Guide*
© 1994 Contemporary Books
A Reproducible Exercise Page

ALOHA!

(PAGES 47–59)

Pre-Reading Activities

Discussion Questions

1. About Hawaii: Have you ever been to Hawaii? What island or islands did you visit? What did you do there? How long did it take you to get there? Have you ever seen pictures of Hawaii? What did you notice in the pictures? What have you heard about Hawaii?

2. About islands: What islands have you visited? Can you think of an island that's a major U.S. city? Why do people like to vacation on islands?

3. About geologic time: The Hawaiian Islands are 25 million years old, yet they are "babies." We call them babies because the continents are 300 million years old. How is geologic time different from everyday time? At what age do you consider people old?

4. About volcanoes: Have you ever seen a volcano or pictures of a volcano? How do volcanoes change the landscape of a place?

5. About mythology: Maui and Pele are used to explain how the Hawaiian Islands were formed. Do you know any myths about the United States? Why do people use myths? How are myths like superstitions? How are they different?

6. About Hawaii: (The last two states to be admitted to the United States, Hawaii and Alaska, are very different from each other in climate. Using the photo of Hawaii that opens this chapter and what students know about Alaska, have them list those differences.)

7. About the teaser: Which islands are actually the crests of an underwater mountain range? (The answer is in paragraph 3. Discuss the fact that what we see of islands is only part of the story. Tell students to imagine looking underwater at the Hawaiian Islands.) What would you see?

8. About the opening paragraph: How does Hawaiian myth explain how the area became all islands? Would it be better if Hawaii was one land mass? In what ways is it easier to live on a large piece of land than on an island?

Section Headings

Ask students the following questions regarding headings and subheads:

"Maui and Pele": Who are Maui and Pele?

"East Meets West": How does east meet west in Hawaii?

"The Tourists Are Coming!": Could this section be headed "The Economy of Hawaii"?

"Hawaiian Pleasures": What are some Hawaiian pleasures?

"Sacrifices and Courage": To what event in World War II history does this subhead refer?

Important Vocabulary from the Reading

1. Have students scan the reading for important words about nature and geography: *islands, atolls, cliffs, volcanoes, craters,* and *lava.*

2. Have students notice Hawaiian words in the reading: *aloha, leis, ukuleles, luaus, hula, onolicious,* and *poi.* Ask students if they know any other words used in English that originally come from other languages.

Activities to Accompany the Reading

Playing Word Games

1. Have students scan the reading for adjectives. Ask them questions in which adjectives are used and/or the answers of which include adjectives. Here are some sample questions: How would you describe Maui's brothers? (They were *curious.*) Are the volcanoes in the national park *noisy* or *quiet*? (They are *quiet.*)

2. The hula was once used to tell stories of Hawaiian history. In that way, it is like the modern game Charades. Divide the class into two teams. Have them play Charades to guess the important vocabulary words in the chapter such as *hula, luau, aloha, taboo, sacrifice, volcano,* and *island.*

Improvising Scenes

1. Have students act as Maui and his brothers. Have Maui warn his brothers not to be curious. Then have students tell the consequences of the brothers' curiosity.

2. Have students act as Pele and her sister. Have them argue with each other: "If you throw lava on me, I'll cause a storm to blow the sea on you," etc.

3. Have students pretend that they are going to Hawaii. Have them tell the travel agent all the things they want to see and do.

Summarizing the Text

Have students describe a visit to Hawaii Volcanoes National Park or the U.S.S. Arizona memorial.

Using Maps

Have students locate the five major islands on a map. Have them find Pearl Harbor, Honolulu, and Waikiki Beach.

Studying Word Parts

The Hawaiian word *onolicious* contains the word part *-ious*, which can mean "characterized by" or "full of." Ask students the following: What words contain this word part? (*delicious, nutritious, judicious, suspicious*) What do these words mean?

Reading for Details

Ask students to reread About the Islands on the Sidelights page. Have them identify the nicknames of each of the five major islands.

Discussion, Writing, or Research Topics

Have students select one of the following topics, do library research on it, and work with classmates to prepare a group presentation for the class.

- Maui and Pele
- volcanoes
- how Hawaii became a state
- Polynesia

- Tahiti
- Captain James Cook
- Kilauea
- the pineapple industry
- surfing
- history of the hula
- Hawaiian foods
- Father Damien
- Pearl Harbor

Extension Activities

1. Bring in some Hawaiian music. Play it for the students.

2. Take a tour of a natural history museum that has an exhibit on the culture of the South Pacific.

3. Bring in books or travel films with photos of Hawaii and show them to the class.

4. Read excerpts to the class from James Michener's novel *Hawaii.*

5. Bring in books or videotapes about the bombing of Pearl Harbor and show them to the class.

For ESL Students

1. Have students say the following groups of words aloud:

   island / eyelet
   volcanoes / canoes
   coral / choral / chore

2. Have students notice that the word *separate* is pronounced differently depending on whether it's being used as an adjective or a verb. Have them pronounce the words in the following sentences:

   - They took *separate* vacations to Hawaii this year.

   - Can you *separate* fact from fiction about how the islands formed?

3. The reading contains the phrasal verb *killed by*, "killed by the eruption of the volcano." Ask students how the phrasal verb *killed for* is connected to the idea of sacrifice.

READING COMPREHENSION

A. Mark each of these statements *True* or *False*.

_____ **1.** The Hawaiian Islands are the tip of the biggest mountain range on Earth.

_____ **2.** Tahitians came to Hawaii 2000 years ago.

_____ **3.** Captain James Cook was a god of peace and fertility.

_____ **4.** The Hawaiian tourist industry grew after World War II.

_____ **5.** In the 16th century, there was a taboo against basket weaving.

B. Complete these statements.

1. According to legend, Hawaii is a series of islands because _____
_____.

2. Pele hid in a crater because _____.

3. Priests sacrificed plants and animals because _____
_____.

4. Tourism became more popular after World War II because _____
_____.

5. Missionaries outlawed the hula because _____
_____.

6. The Hawaiian luau features foods from many different countries because _____
_____.

7. Only part of the U.S.S. Arizona memorial can be seen because _____
_____.

BOOK 3

READING COMPREHENSION (CONTINUED)

C. Circle the letter of the best answer to complete each sentence.

1. The main idea of paragraph 12 is stated in (a) the first sentence (b) the last sentence (c) no sentence in the paragraph.

2. According to paragraph 14, Hawaii became a popular tourist attraction for (a) one reason (b) three reasons (c) no reason that's given.

3. According to paragraph 16, shopping is (a) the main reason for people to come to Hawaii (b) less popular than sunning and surfing (c) the nation's oldest sport.

4. According to paragraph 19, the hula can be practiced (a) only by islanders (b) by islanders and tourists (c) only at universities.

5. According to paragraph 26, Diamond Head (a) was named by Hawaiian natives (b) is an accurate name for the crater (c) is an inaccurate name for the crater.

D. Circle the numbers of all of the sentences that are true about paragraph 26.

1. It contrasts two names for Diamond Head.

2. It describes Diamond Head.

3. It takes the reader on a tour of Diamond Head.

4. It provides some history about Diamond Head.

5. It gives the location of Diamond Head.

6. It compares Diamond Head to other volcanic craters.

ATTRACTIONS *Teacher's Guide*
© 1994 Contemporary Books
A Reproducible Exercise Page

VOCABULARY PRACTICE

A. Use some of these words to complete the sentences that follow.

atolls	lava	scholars	ukuleles
geologic	migrations	stunts	volcanoes
hike	publicized	surfers	weave
islands	remote	typical	wrinkled

1. Pele is described as a _____ old woman.

2. Sailors followed bird _____ to find their way in the ocean.

3. After World War II, soldiers _____ the beauty of Hawaii.

4. Hula _____ study the traditions of the dance.

5. Only birds and small creatures can live on _____.

6. Sometimes at luaus, musicians strum _____.

7. _____ time is different from historical time.

B. Match each place or thing in the column on the left with an adjective in the column on the right that describes it in the reading. Write the correct letters on the blank lines.

_____ 1. cliff   **(a)** athletic

_____ 2. museum   **(b)** living

_____ 3. coast   **(c)** lonely

_____ 4. waters   **(d)** beautiful

_____ 5. tourists   **(e)** southern

_____ 6. main islands   **(f)** fatal

_____ 7. lava flow   **(g)** five

BOOK 3

WORDS IN CONTEXT

What does each word mean in the paragraph indicated? Reread the paragraphs. Then circle the letter of the correct answer.

1. <u>crests</u> (teaser): (a) helmets (b) the tops of something

2. <u>basins</u> (6): (a) bowls for holding liquid (b) bowl-shaped depressions in the Earth

3. <u>erupted</u> (11): (a) exploded (b) pierced the skin

4. <u>instrument</u> (14): (a) a device for producing music (b) a mechanical device

5. <u>features</u> (19): (a) gives special attention to (b) resembles

HOMONYMS, SYNONYMS, AND SIMILAR WORDS

A. Match each word in the column on the left with the correct word or phrase in the column on the right. Write the correct letter on the blank lines.

_____ 1. tragic   **(a)** display

_____ 2. fascinating   **(b)** played music on strings

_____ 3. strummed   **(c)** brought from elsewhere

_____ 4. imported   **(d)** very interesting

_____ 5. exhibit   **(e)** disastrous, terrible

B. Complete these sentences using the homonyms provided correctly.

1. If we stay on that side of the island, will we be able to _____ the _____?
(sea / see)

2. At the ancient temples, the priests made sacrifices to assure good _____.
Sometimes people were sacrificed _____ they agreed or not.
(whether / weather)

ATTRACTIONS *Teacher's Guide*
© 1994 Contemporary Books
A Reproducible Exercise Page

PATTERN PRACTICE

Rewrite these sentences, connecting each pair of sentences with the word *because*.

1. Hawaii became separate islands. Maui's brothers looked back.

   _____

2. Hawaii is a mere baby. Some of it is only 200 years old.

   _____

3. Natives worshipped Captain Cook. They thought he was a god.

   _____

4. Pele went from crater to crater. She was trying to escape her sister.

   _____

5. People were punished. They broke taboos.

   _____

PARTS OF SPEECH AND INFLECTED FORMS

Complete these sentences with the proper verb forms of the underlined phrases.

1. Frank likes to surf. Yesterday he _____ on Diamond Head.

2. Carla likes to make leis. Tomorrow she _____ _____ a lei out of orchids.

3. Many tourists like to dance the hula. _____ you _____ the hula at the hotel last night?

4. Believe it or not, some people like to ski in Hawaii. _____ you ever _____ on the island?

5. People used to weave baskets on the island. _____ she ever _____ a basket before?

BOOK 3

WORD PARTS

Study the meanings of these words from the reading. Then use some of them to complete the sentences that follow.

discover	geologic	inhabitants	television
elevation	imported	involved	variety

1. Tourists find a _____ of sports to entertain them.

2. The _____ of Hawaii come from many diverse cultures.

3. In _____ time, Hawaii is a baby.

4. After World War II, _____ personalities publicized Hawaii.

5. One of the volcanoes has a higher _____ than the other.

PHRASAL VERBS AND OTHER IDIOMS

Reread the paragraphs that the phrases in the column on the left are used in. Then match each phrase with its definition in the column on the right. Write the correct letters on the blank lines.

_____ 1. came from (9)   **(a)** characterize

_____ 2. describe as (7)   **(b)** made available

_____ 3. killed by (11)   **(c)** lost life by means of

_____ 4. opened the (12)   **(d)** told in music accompanied by words

_____ 5. sang about (14)   **(e)** originated in

_____ 6. stay for (6)   **(f)** remain a certain amount of time

ATTRACTIONS *Teacher's Guide*
© 1994 Contemporary Books
A Reproducible Exercise Page

LA LA LAND

(PAGES 63–73)

Pre-Reading Activities

Discussion Questions

1. About California: How does it rank in area and population compared to the other states? (The answers are on the Sidelights page.) What are its major cities? Have you ever been there? Tell your impressions.

2. About Los Angeles: Los Angeles is the name of the city, the county, and the five-county metropolitan area. How does the city rank nationally in population? What are some of the area's problems that have attracted national attention in recent years? What are some famous sites there?

3. About Hollywood: Is it a separate city or just a section of a city? What do tourists come here to see? What is its major industry?

4. About movies: Which do you prefer, American movies or foreign films? Why? What's your favorite American movie? Who's your favorite movie star?

5. About the title: What does the reading's title refer to? Of course, the letters *LA* are the initials of Los Angeles. But, in addition, what does the term *la la* suggest?

6. About the photographs accompanying the reading: Have you seen the Hollywood sign in other photographs? Note the photograph of the Walk of Fame. Would you like to be a famous entertainer and be honored in this way? Would you pay $5,000 to have a star named for you?

7. About the teaser: What tradition might have been started by a movie star's stepping in the wrong place? (Paragraph 9 gives the answer.)

Section Headings

"Hollywoodland": Ask students what the word part *land* in this heading suggests. It calls to mind an imaginary, magical, wonderful place, such as the kind that exist in children's stories.

"Hollywood History": Ask students how they expect ideas to be organized in this section. A history is usually presented chronologically.

"Star Search": Ask students who's searching and for what kind of stars.

"City of Angels": This heading is what *Los Angeles* means in Spanish. It may be viewed as ironic considering the city's high crime rate.

Important Vocabulary from the Reading

1. Discuss phrases from the reading including *entertainment medium, stunt show,* and *overcrowded and underfunded.*

2. Define the words *dominate, durable, enamel,* and *industry.*

3. Read aloud *celebrity, threaten,* and *mezzanine.*

4. Distinguish between the following pairs of words:

business / industry	mezzanine / balcony
deceased / diseased	major / minor
band / bandshell	home / estate
highway / freeway	county / community
fog / smog	casual / formal
celebrity / star	celebrity / fan

Activities to Accompany the Reading

Playing Word Games

Write the list below on the chalkboard. Have students write the noun for the descriptions of people listed. The answers follow.

1. is famous 2. performs for an audience 3. admires a performer 4. can toss and catch three balls at once 5. rides a board on ocean waves 6. lives in a particular place 7. rides a horse and rounds up cattle 8. rides in a moving vehicle 9. buys things in a store 10. is new to a place or group 11. plays a musical instrument 12. lives in Los Angeles

Answers: 1. celebrity or star 2. performer or entertainer 3. fan 4. juggler 5. surfer 6. resident 7. cowboy 8. passenger 9. customer 10. newcomer 11. musician 12. Angeleno

Improvising Scenes

Have pairs of students act out their favorite scene from a recent movie. Then have the class guess the names of the movies.

Comparing and Contrasting

1. Have students compare L.A. to the city they live in. Ask them what the advantages and disadvantages of each place are.

2. Have students make figurative comparisons. Ask them how a movie star is like a star in the sky.

Using Maps

1. On a U.S. map, have students find the major cities in California.

2. Study maps of California and of Los Angeles to find the names of the various places mentioned in the reading (Beverly Hills, Hollywood, Venice, San Diego, etc.).

Discussion, Writing, or Research Topics

1. After they've read a few travel books in the library, have students write a paragraph or short composition about the southern California tourist site they'd most like to visit.

2. Have students read a biography, autobiography, or interview with some celebrity they admire. Then have them tell the class some interesting, little-known facts about that celebrity.

Extension Activities

1. Have the students select four good movies that are currently playing in town or are available on videotape. Then have each student choose one of the four movies to view. Allow a week's time for everyone to see the movie. Then divide the students into four groups and have them discuss, evaluate, and write a group movie review. They might divide the writing up into various components of the film, such as acting, directing, photography, plot, setting, music, special effects, and costumes.

2. Have students write short movie scenes. Videotape the student scenes, and show them in class. The scenes might have a unifying theme such as crime, family life, the working world, or finding humor in everyday life.

For ESL Students

1. Ask which one is bigger in each pair:

   an ocean / a lake
   a mile / a block
   a business / an industry
   a hill / a mountain
   a shop / a shopping center
   a neighborhood / a city

2. Ask each student to report on a movie or TV show he or she saw recently.

3. Ask students to compare and contrast American movies and those made in their native countries. Have them consider the types of plots, special effects, acting, sets, costumes, and amount of violence.

4. What does the word part -graph mean? What is a phonograph, a photograph, an autograph? What are graphics? Discuss the meanings of these words.

READING COMPREHENSION

A. Mark each of these statements *True* or *False*.

_____ **1.** The Wax Museum is a meeting place for movie stars.

_____ **2.** Rodeo Drive is in Hollywood.

_____ **3.** An American movie star doesn't have much privacy.

_____ **4.** Hollywood is in the city of Los Angeles.

_____ **5.** A county is one section of a city.

B. Complete these sentences with information from the reading.

1. Southern California is a good place to make movies because _____
_____.

2. Los Angeles tourists go to see movie stars' homes because _____
_____.

3. Movie stars want to win an Oscar because _____
_____.

4. Some people don't like Los Angeles because _____
_____.

C. Number these places 1–8 from smallest to largest in area.

_____ the city of Los Angeles

_____ the Southwest

_____ Hollywood

_____ California

_____ Hollywood Boulevard

_____ southern California

_____ the county of Los Angeles

_____ the Hollywood Bowl

BOOK 3

READING COMPREHENSION (CONTINUED)

D. Circle the item that doesn't belong in each group.

1. <u>traditions for movie fans</u>: reading the stars' names along the Walk of Fame, being photographed in front of the Hollywood sign, photographing the footprints in front of the Chinese Theater, watching the Academy Awards on TV

2. <u>scenery on the West Coast</u>: the Pacific Ocean, mountains, earthquakes, hills

3. <u>disadvantages of living in Los Angeles</u>: beautiful scenery, high crime rate, heavy traffic, expensive homes

4. <u>substances you can make footprints in</u>: sand, wood, mud, wet cement

E. Number these events 1–7 in the order that they happened. Start with the one that happened first.

_____ Hollywood became the center of the American movie industry.

_____ The movie projector was invented.

_____ The first talking movie was made.

_____ Silent movies were shown in movie theaters.

_____ The Hollywoodland sign was built.

_____ The first Academy Awards were given.

_____ The first full-length film was produced.

ATTRACTIONS *Teacher's Guide*
© 1994 Contemporary Books
A Reproducible Exercise Page

VOCABULARY PRACTICE

Use some of these words to fill in the blanks in the paragraphs that follow.

autograph	earthquake	perform	scenery
climate	floods	photographs	tourist
coast	highways	pile	traffic
curiosity	outstanding	resident	waves

(1) I recommend southern California as an _____ area to live in. (2) If you like mountains and the ocean, you'll love the _____ in southern California. (3) The ocean is fun to swim in, especially when the _____ are high. (4) If you like warm, sunny weather, you'll enjoy the _____.

Of course, southern California is not a perfect place. (5) When there's an _____ and your furniture begins to shake, that's scary. (6) No one wants his home to turn into a _____ of bricks. (7) And when the rainy season comes, there can be _____ and mud slides. Those aren't fun, either.

(8) Come to southern California for a visit. Start out by being a _____ here. (9) Then you can satisfy your _____ about the area. (10) When the weather is nice, it's great to drive along the Pacific _____. (11) You'll want to bring your camera and take a lot of _____. (12) If you fall in love with the West Coast, then you can become a _____. (13) Everyone else is doing it. Pretty soon, southern California will have to build _____ underground to prevent _____ jams.

BOOK 3

WORDS IN CONTEXT

What do the underlined phrases mean in this reading? Reread the paragraphs. Then circle the letter of each correct answer.

1. In paragraph 4, <u>all over</u> means (a) everywhere (b) finished (c) broken.

2. In paragraph 21, <u>ethnic neighborhoods</u> means (a) areas with honest residents (b) areas with poor residents (c) areas where most residents have the same cultural background.

3. In paragraph 22, the phrase <u>traffic jams</u> means that cars are (a) moving very slowly (b) traveling above the speed limit (c) in an accident.

4. Paragraph 22 says that L.A. has high <u>unemployment</u>; that means that (a) a lot of people don't want to work (b) many people who want to work can't find jobs (c) there are very few businesses in the area.

5. In paragraph 22, <u>get stuck</u> means to (a) be unable to move (b) be cheated (c) be stabbed.

6. In paragraph 23, <u>handout</u> means (a) offering to shake hands (b) a donation (c) a signal to stop.

HOMONYMS, SYNONYMS, AND SIMILAR WORDS

Find a word that defines these words or phrases by scanning the paragraphs indicated. Write the synonyms on the lines.

1. <u>long-lasting</u> (3) _____

2. <u>smoke and fog</u> (3) _____

3. <u>well-known people</u> (10, 17) _____

4. <u>something people come to see</u> (11) _____

5. <u>signatures obtained as souvenirs</u> (12) _____

ATTRACTIONS *Teacher's Guide*
© 1994 Contemporary Books
A Reproducible Exercise Page

PATTERN PRACTICE

Read the first sentence in paragraph 5 and the first sentence in paragraph 24. In each sentence, a colon is used to mean "namely" or "for example." Complete these sentences with information from the reading.

1. Hollywood has many interesting tourist attractions: _____
   _____ .

2. In Hollywood, tourists can see many different types of movies: _____
   _____ .

3. Visitors to Los Angeles search for movie stars in many different places: _____
   _____ .

PARTS OF SPEECH AND INFLECTED FORMS

Complete these sentences using appropriate past participles to complete the passive-voice verbs. Look in the reading for help, if necessary.

Example: Open-air concerts are <u>held</u> in the Hollywood Bowl.

1. Most early silent films were _____ in Chicago.

2. Talking movies were _____ in 1927.

3. By the 1930s, American movie stars were _____ worldwide.

4. The Hollywoodland sign was _____ in 1923.

5. On Universal Studio's train ride, passengers are _____ by a shark and an earthquake.

6. The names of Oscar winners are _____ secret until the awards are
   _____ .

BOOK 3

WORD PARTS

Complete each sentence with a word beginning with *under-* or *over-*.

over- = above, too much   *under-* = not enough

1. It's too expensive. It's _____priced.

2. There are too many people living there. It's _____crowded.

3. He's very happy. In fact, he's _____joyed.

4. She's too thin. She needs to gain weight. She's _____weight.

5. He's smart, but he gets poor grades. He's an _____achiever.

6. He didn't wake up on time. He _____slept.

PHRASAL VERBS AND OTHER IDIOMS

Complete the sentences that follow using some of these idioms from the reading.

fall in love with	keep a secret	show its age
gets stuck	no wonder	takes (something) in stride
handout	run-down	traffic jam

1. John studies very hard. It's _____ _____ he gets good grades.

2. He goes to school and works part time. But he _____ his heavy schedule _____ _____ .

3. When he gets stuck in a _____ _____, he studies on the freeway.

4. When he _____ _____ and can't do a math problem, he goes to a tutor for help.

5. He supports himself. He won't take a _____ from his relatives.

ATTRACTIONS *Teacher's Guide*
© 1994 Contemporary Books
A Reproducible Exercise Page

WINTER WONDERLAND

(PAGES 77–85)

Pre-Reading Activities

Discussion Questions

1. About Minnesota: Where is Minnesota? What do you think the climate is like there? What do you know about the state? What is it well known for?

2. About malls: Do you have malls in your city or town? What kinds of stores are there? Why do shoppers like malls?

3. About Paul Bunyan: Can you describe Paul Bunyan? What did he look like? What was his occupation? What animal was his constant companion? Was he a real or a fictitious character? Do you know any tall tales about him?

4. About the Peanuts comic strip: Who are the important characters? Can you describe their personalities and interests? What does the name of the comic strip mean? Are there ever any adult characters in this comic strip? Whose dog is Snoopy? Does Snoopy behave like most dogs?

5. About the title: Do you know the song "Winter Wonderland"? What turns a walk on a winter day into a visit to wonderland? Recalling the book *Alice in Wonderland*, what does the word *wonderland* suggest?

6. About the photographs: What impression of Minnesota do you get from the photos?

7. About the teaser: What do you think Minneapolis's coldest temperature was? (The answer is −59°F.)

Section Headings

"Icebox, U.S.A.": Ask students if they think this is the name of a real city. When they read the section, they'll discover that it refers to International Falls, Minnesota. But the section covers other Minnesota cold spots as well.

"Outdoor Sports Move Indoors": This section is about the Metrodome, an indoor stadium. Discuss some sports that are traditionally played outdoors. Ask if anyone has ever watched or played one of these sports indoors. Ask if it increases or decreases the fans' enjoyment.

"Mall of America": Ask students what they expect to learn about the mall in this section. Possible answers include where it is, why it's important and/or interesting, what's in the mall, and when it was built. Make a list of expected information. Then have students read the section and check off the information they find.

"That's Entertainment": The story of Mall of America continues in this section. Here, the emphasis is upon its recreational facilities.

Important Vocabulary from the Reading

1. Discuss vocabulary of the business world including *retailers*, *vendors*, *bargain*, and *developers*. Define *retailer*. Introduce and define *wholesaler*.

2. Have students pronounce *extraordinary* [ex•troar'din•air•ee] and *kiosk* [key'ahsk]. These words may be new to students.

3. The word *complex* is used as a noun in this chapter (in the phrase *a movie complex*). Discuss its meaning as an adjective and its relationship to the adjectives *complex* and *complicated*.

4. Discuss the difference in meaning between *weather* and *climate*.

Activities to Accompany the Reading

Playing Word Games

Play this timed game with partners or teams. Have students list as many words as possible containing the letter combination -*all*. There are many in this reading (water*fall*, m*all*, etc.). Students get two points for each -*all* word from the reading, one point each for others.

Improvising Scenes

Tell students that tall tales about Paul Bunyan were made up by loggers sitting around a campfire at night. The stories described a man with great strength and clever (and impossible) solutions to problems. For example, one story tells of Paul straightening a winding river by giving its tail a yank. Have students pretend they are sitting around a campfire, entertaining one another with tall tales about Paul and Babe. See who can come up with the most exaggerated and impossible incident. Students who have difficulty inventing their own stories may tell one they have read. As a variation, have one student begin a tall tale about Paul, and then ask each person in the circle to add a sentence or two.

Comparing and Contrasting

Have students compare and contrast (orally or in writing) the Metrodome and a conventional open-air stadium.

Using Maps

Point out Minnesota on a map of the United States. Then have students find Minneapolis and St. Paul. Ask why they're called the Twin Cities. Have students locate Bloomington, Duluth, International Falls, the Mississippi River, and Lake Itasca. Ask students how many of the state's lakes they can see on the map. If possible, get a map of Minnesota to show how many of the state's lakes appear there.

Studying Word Parts

Discuss word parts *mega-* and *metro-*. Ask students what words they know that contain these word parts.

Using Math

Change −49°F to a Celsius temperature. Celsius equals Fahrenheit minus 32, divided by 1.8. The answer is −45°C.

Discussion, Writing, or Research Topics

1. Have students research Paul Bunyan and other legendary characters from American folklore and tell about them in class. Some names to recommend include Casey Jones, John Henry, Davey Crockett, Mike Fink, Jesse James, and Billy the Kid. Write them on the board. Ask students which ones were real people and which were fictitious.

2. Discuss the typical American mall. Ask students the following: What are some things that malls do to attract customers and keep them there as long as possible? Are malls dangerous? Have you heard of any crimes committed at malls?

Extension Activities

1. Play some songs from the Broadway musical "You're a Good Man, Charlie Brown." The show was based upon the Peanuts comic strip.

2. *Spoonbridge and Cherry* (mentioned on the Sidelights page) was created by Claes Oldenburg and his wife, Coosje Van Bruggen. Find some photographs of this and other work by these artists, and show them in class. Students will enjoy Oldenburg's giant baseball bat. A man dressed in a Batman costume once climbed this sculpture.

For ESL Students

To help ESL students develop listening skills and the ability to use short answers and pronouns, ask the following questions:

- Is Babe an ox or a dog?
- Is Snoopy a dog or a cat?
- Is a bargain expensive or cheap?
- Was Paul Bunyan real or fictional?
- Are the Minnesota Twins an amateur or professional team?
- Is a rectangle a type of square?
- Are the winters in Minnesota cold or warm?
- Are there any nightclubs in Mall of America?
- Do fish swim in an aquarium or a stadium?
- Is there a theme park in Mall of America?
- Was Paul Bunyan strong or weak?

READING COMPREHENSION

A. Mark each of these statements *True* or *False*.

_____ **1.** West Edmonton Mall is about the same size as Mall of America.

_____ **2.** Mall of America has more shops than restaurants.

_____ **3.** Paul Bunyan's companion was an ox named Babe.

_____ **4.** The Twin Cities are Bloomington and Minneapolis.

_____ **5.** Knott's Camp Snoopy is outdoors.

B. Complete these sentences.

1. The little town of International Falls, Minnesota, is often in the news because _____.

2. The Metrodome was needed in Minnesota because _____.

3. Knott's Camp Snoopy can stay open even when _____.

4. The Metrodome is used for many different sports because _____.

5. Space for Mall of America became available when _____.

6. Mall of America has been good for the area's economy because _____.

7. Minneapolis and St. Paul _____.

8. The Metrodome is unusual because _____.

BOOK 3

READING COMPREHENSION (CONTINUED)

C. Circle the letter of the best answer to complete each sentence.

1. According to this reading, Minnesota residents cope with cold winters by
(a) staying indoors nearly all the time (b) going to Florida for three months
(c) entertaining themselves with both indoor and outdoor activities.

2. The information in paragraph 3 gives (a) the reasons for having a festival such as
Icebox Days (b) examples of various competitions held during Icebox Days (c) the
history of Icebox Days.

3. According to paragraphs 6–9, baseball and football (a) can be played outdoors only
(b) are warm-weather sports (c) can be played either indoors or outdoors.

4. According to paragraphs 13–14, the retailers of the Twin Cities were (a) eager for
Mall of America to be built (b) fearful of competition from Mall of America
(c) disappointed that it wasn't the largest mall in the world.

5. In paragraph 20, the number of reasons given to explain why Camp Snoopy seems
to be outdoors is (a) two (b) three (c) four.

D. Scan the paragraphs indicated in the reading to find the following information:

1. the height of the Winter Carnival's 1992 Ice Castle (5): _____

2. the number of people the Metrodome can seat for baseball (9): _____

3. the number of major department stores at the mall (16): _____

4. the approximate number of shops at the mall (16): _____

5. the number of workers employed by the mall (23): _____

ATTRACTIONS *Teacher's Guide*
© 1994 Contemporary Books
A Reproducible Exercise Page

VOCABULARY PRACTICE

A. Use some of these words to complete the sentences that follow.

amateur	extraordinary	namesake	severe
cancel	frigid	obstacles	transform
corridor	humor	retailers	vacant
dome	kiosk	scouts	vendor

1. Merchants who sell goods directly to users of the product are _____.

2. A _____ winter brings frigid weather.

3. Barriers that prevent someone from achieving a goal are _____.

4. Now that there's an indoor stadium in St. Paul, it is rarely necessary to postpone or _____ sporting events.

5. Mall of America is an _____ mall because it's so big.

6. _____ athletes don't get paid for playing a sport.

B. Match each item in the column on the left with the material it's made of in the column on the right. Write the correct letters on the blank lines.

_____ 1. beach   **(a)** fiberglass

_____ 2. Lego blocks   **(b)** glass

_____ 3. log   **(c)** plastic

_____ 4. Metrodome ceiling   **(d)** artificial grass

_____ 5. Metrodome floor   **(e)** wood

_____ 6. skylight   **(f)** sand

BOOK 3

WORDS IN CONTEXT

What does each word mean in the paragraph indicated? Reread the paragraphs. Then circle the letter of the correct answer.

1. <u>current</u> (2): (a) water or air flowing in the same direction (b) something happening now

2. <u>sponsor</u> (3): (a) pays for a particular activity (b) has a lot of interests

3. <u>brave</u> (4): (a) courageous, heroic (b) endure, put up with, go out in

4. <u>converted</u> (8): (a) changed (b) reduced in size

5. <u>unique</u> (23): (a) unusual (b) one of a kind

HOMONYMS, SYNONYMS, AND SIMILAR WORDS

A. Match each word in the column on the left with the correct word or phrase from the column on the right. Write the correct letters on the blank lines.

_____ 1. amateur

_____ 2. artificial

_____ 3. gigantic

_____ 4. lumberjack

_____ 5. stadium

(a) fake, not the original, not real

(b) not professional, not paid for the activity

(c) logger

(d) sports arena

(e) huge

B. Complete these sentences using the homonyms provided correctly.

1. I don't know _____ the _____ will be rainy or sunny tomorrow.
    (weather / whether)

2. At the _____ of the accident, we saw a terrible _____.
    (sight / site)

ATTRACTIONS *Teacher's Guide*
© 1994 Contemporary Books
A Reproducible Exercise Page

PATTERN PRACTICE

Rewrite these sentences inserting the word *and* in the correct place.

1. Mall of America is a place for shopping entertainment.

_____

2. The mall has stores, a miniature golf course, restaurants, nightclubs.

_____

3. Paul Bunyan could pull a tree out of the ground with his bare hands break it in half.

_____

4. The Metrodome is used for amateur professional sports.

_____

PARTS OF SPEECH AND INFLECTED FORMS

Rewrite these phrases using a past participle as an adjective. For help, reread the paragraphs indicated.

Example: a park with a lot of plants (15): <u>a landscaped park</u>

1. roof with a dome (7): _____

2. store owners who are concerned (14): _____

3. merchandise that costs a lot (16): _____

4. a theme park that's indoors (17): _____

5. passengers that are sitting down (18): _____

BOOK 3

WORD PARTS

Use these word parts to complete the sentences that follow.

> *inter-* = between, among, with each other
> *mega-* = large, great, powerful
> *metro-* = measure, mother (also used to mean "city")
> *sub-* = under

1. Highways that go from one state to another are _____state highways.

2. A _____phone makes a person's voice louder.

3. Ships that travel under the water are called _____marines.

4. A _____polis is a big city.

PHRASAL VERBS AND OTHER IDIOMS

Reread the paragraphs these phrasal verbs are used in. The paragraph numbers are in parentheses. Then use some of the phrasal verbs to complete the sentences that follow.

> get tired of (6)   scale down (14)
> come up with (11)   team up with (14)
> go along with (13)   try out (16)

1. Before you buy a car, you should _____ it _____ by taking it for a test drive.

2. I don't like your plan. I just can't _____ it.

3. Let's brainstorm. Maybe we can _____ another idea.

4. I can't manage this store alone. I need to _____ a partner.

5. Do you ever _____ being a student?

ATTRACTIONS *Teacher's Guide*
© 1994 Contemporary Books
A Reproducible Exercise Page

EARTH MOTHER

(PAGES 3–13)

Pre-Reading Activities

Discussion Questions

1. About Maryland: What do you know about the state? What states border it? What important city borders it?

2. About Washington, D.C.: What important government buildings are in Washington, D.C.? Have you ever visited our nation's capital? What do the important buildings and monuments look like? What is the difference between a building and a monument?

3. About pesticides: What is a pesticide? What is DDT? What was it designed to do? What harmful effects have we found DDT to cause?

4. About ecology: (Earth Day, recycling, "green" products—all are relatively new ideas.) What do you know about ecology? How is your life influenced by ecology?

5. About Rachel Carson's writing career: Is it very unusual for a scientist to be a bestselling author? Do you know of any other science writers? Do you like to read about science and nature? What subject in science and nature would interest you?

6. About the title: Why is Carson called Earth Mother? Have you heard the expression "mother earth"? What does it mean?

7. About the photographs: What impression do you get of Carson from the photographs? What kind of woman was she?

8. About the teaser: What new field of science came about because of one woman's study of nature? (As the reading explains, Carson's work led to the field of ecology.)

Section Headings

"A Natural Writer": Ask students what it means to be a natural writer. Point out the early age that Carson began writing. Also point out the pun: *natural writer* versus *nature writer*.

"Hardship and Triumph": This part of the chapter discusses how personal losses and world events made Carson's life as a professional writer and scientist difficult. Ask students what the personal events were and what the world events were. Students might be encouraged to guess the world events from the dates provided.

"A Quiet Fighter": Ask students the following: Does a person have to be loud or shrill to be convincing? What was Carson fighting for?

"Honors and Awards": This section discusses Carson's triumphs and recognition for her work.

"Tributes and Landmarks": Have students skim the section and then name the three landmarks dedicated to Carson.

Important Vocabulary from the Reading

1. Discuss the science vocabulary included in the reading: *biology, research, chemicals, microscopes, pesticide, environment, ecosystem, toxic, synthetics, EPA,* and *wildlife refuge.*

2. Discuss some of the names, positive and negative, that people called Carson: "pioneer," "nature lover," "bird lover," "hysterical woman," and "genius."

3. Discuss terms that relate to publishing including *bestseller, published, children's magazine, articles, booklets,* and *illustrated book.*

Activities to Accompany the Reading

Playing Word Games

1. Have students make a list of all the nouns in the chapter that name what Carson was. See who has the most items on his or her list. Then ask students to add to the list with names of their own.

2. Have students work in a team to make lists of all the scientific inventions that have helped humankind. Have another team think of all the scientific inventions that have hurt humankind.

Improvising Scenes

1. Have students pretend that they are the young Carson convincing her brother that hunting is wrong. Have other students disagree at first by providing reasons for hunting.

2. Have students pretend that they are Carson talking on the phone to her friend Olga Owens Huckins after receiving the letter about her bird sanctuary. Have students tell her how they plan to help her.

3. Have students pretend that they are giving Carson the "Woman of the Year" Award. Have them list her accomplishments.

Comparing and Contrasting

1. Have students compare Carson's interests and accomplishments as a child with her interests and accomplishments as an adult.

2. Have students contrast how people viewed nature before and after the "invention" of ecology.

Using Maps

1. On a map of Maryland, have students find Silver Spring and Baltimore, the location of Johns Hopkins University.

2. Have students find Pennsylvania and Maine on a map of the United States.

Discussion, Writing, or Research Topics

1. Have students research the ecology movement. Have them report on Carson's contribution.

2. Have students research the use of pesticides versus the growing interest in organic farming.

3. Have students look at Carson's published works and read parts of them. Both *Silent Spring* and *The Sea Around Us* are beautifully written. Provide students with a chapter from each to read and discuss.

4. Provide students with book reviews or news stories pertaining to *Silent Spring*. Show them how people were divided on the subject. Ask them to evaluate a few opposing articles.

5. Provide students with Carson's *New York Times* obituary. Have them discuss it. Ask if they learned anything new from it.

6. Have two teams of four students each debate the statement "Because scientific discoveries can harm humankind, potentially damaging research should be stopped." Have them provide examples.

Extension Activities

1. Take students to a science or natural history museum, botanical garden, or zoo. Have them tour the ecology exhibits.

2. Have a member of an ecology group lecture the students about the environmental movement.

3. Bring in a popular ecology book like *50 Ways You Can Help to Save the Planet*. Discuss some of its ideas with the students. Have students add ideas of their own.

4. Have students draw up a proposal for an ecology project in their neighborhoods. If possible, have them develop the proposal into a working plan for recycling, planting a vacant lot, or cleaning up an area of beach.

For ESL Students

Ask students the following questions: Is ecology an issue in their country? Had they heard of Carson? Who are some scientific heroes from their culture? Are pesticides widely used in their country? Do people worry about chemicals and the environment? What is being done?

NAME _____

READING COMPREHENSION

A. Mark each of these statements *True* or *False*.

_____ **1.** Carson's first published story was about a pilot.

_____ **2.** In the 1920s, science was a common field of study for women.

_____ **3.** Because people turned their attention to World War I, Carson's first book sold very poorly.

_____ **4.** The man who invented DDT won the Nobel Prize in 1948.

_____ **5.** Those who followed Carson invented the science of biology.

B. Complete each sentence with a clause that tells why or when.

1. Rachel Carson was often alone as a child because _____

_____.

2. She got involved in outdoor science classes when _____

_____.

3. She stayed on an ocean research ship because _____

_____.

4. She knew that *Silent Spring* would influence people when _____

_____.

5. When she was fifty, Carson adopted her nephew because _____

_____.

6. DDT was used widely by farmers because _____

_____.

7. Friends set up the Rachel Carson Council when _____

_____.

READING COMPREHENSION (CONTINUED)

C. Circle the letter of the best answer to complete each sentence.

1. According to this reading, before Rachel Carson, people didn't understand
(a) the ecology of the planet (b) songbirds (c) the science of biology.

2. The information in paragraph 7 gives (a) the history of the United States
(b) examples of difficulties affecting Carson (c) the effects of those difficulties.

3. Paragraphs 8 and 9 discuss how Carson (a) kept losing her job (b) wanted variety
(c) figured out ways to increase her income.

4. Paragraphs 17 and 18 explain all but the following: (a) why pesticides were used
(b) how DDT enters the ecosystem (c) how Carson got her research published.

5. Paragraphs 30 and 31 discuss (a) the three sites associated with Carson
(b) why people appreciate her (c) her years in college.

D. Scan the reading to find the following information:

1. the amount Carson was paid for her first article: _____

2. how much the job of junior aquatic biologist paid: _____

3. the year of publication of *The Sea Around Us*: _____

4. the year that DDT's inventor won the Nobel Prize: _____

5. how many pounds of pesticides were spread in 1963: _____

6. how long Carson lived in her Silver Spring home: _____

7. the year Carson appeared on a postage stamp: _____

ATTRACTIONS *Teacher's Guide*
© 1994 Contemporary Books
A Reproducible Exercise Page

VOCABULARY PRACTICE

A. Use some of these words to complete the sentences that follow.

aquatic	forcefully	pesticide	sanctuary
argued	invitations	poetic	synthetic
economic	microscope	progress	toxic
environment	mosquitoes	research	tribute

1. People who study underwater life are _____ biologists.

2. When you look at something under a _____, you see things invisible to the naked eye.

3. Dangerous _____ chemicals are harmful to the Earth's ecosystem.

4. Her _____ writing about nature is popular with many readers.

5. Scientific _____ is not always good for humankind.

6. She explained the problem simply and _____.

B. Match each item in the column on the left with the possessive form that describes it in the column on the right. Write the correct words from the reading on the blank lines.

1. _____ nests   robins'

2. _____ magazine (for kids)   friend's

3. _____ beautiful songs   man's

4. _____ world (for males)   children's

5. _____ systems (of animals)   birds'

BOOK 4

WORDS IN CONTEXT

What does each word mean in the paragraph indicated? Reread the paragraphs. Then circle the letter of the correct answer.

1. <u>wing</u> (3): (a) the limb of a bird (b) a structure that keeps flying devices in the air

2. <u>agency</u> (11): (a) an action or operation (b) a business or service

3. <u>recognized</u> (18): (a) accepted the status of a new government (b) became aware of, had knowledge of

4. <u>toxic</u> (23): (a) liquid (b) poisonous

5. <u>vision</u> (25): (a) eyesight (b) intelligence, competence

6. <u>mirrored</u> (31): (a) something worthy of imitation (b) made of mirrors

HOMONYMS, SYNONYMS, AND SIMILAR WORDS

A. Match each word in the column on the left with the correct word or phrase in the column on the right. Write the correct letters on the blank lines.

_____ 1. biology	**(a)** the outdoors, all living things
_____ 2. nature	**(b)** a monetary award for pursuing studies
_____ 3. scholarship	
_____ 4. publicized	**(c)** called to the attention of the public
_____ 5. effects	**(d)** results
	(e) the science of life and life processes

B. Complete these sentences using the homonyms provided.

1. She has _____ a difficult burden. She was _____ in Pennsylvania. (born / borne)

2. The pilot flew the _____ in the war. People liked her _____ and simple way of explaining hard material. (plain / plane)

ATTRACTIONS *Teacher's Guide*
© 1994 Contemporary Books
A Reproducible Exercise Page

PATTERN PRACTICE

Rewrite these sentences, beginning each with an infinitive (*to* + a verb).

Example: Carson wanted to make more money. She began writing in her spare time.
    To make more money, Carson began writing in her spare time.

1. Carson wanted to describe World War I. She wrote a story.

   _____

2. Huckins wanted to tell Carson about the songbirds. Huckins wrote her a letter.

   _____

3. Carson wanted to help her friend and her planet. She wrote about DDT.

   _____

4. The government wanted to learn more about DDT. The government conducted hearings.

   _____

PARTS OF SPEECH AND INFLECTED FORMS

A. These words are adverbs. Use them to complete the sentences that follow.

   also   already   finally   forcefully   quietly

1. Carson _____ convinced her brother not to hunt.

2. She _____ knew her little great-nephew very well.

3. Carson had _____ written several other books.

4. She spoke _____ and _____.

B. You can make some adverbs into adjectives by dropping the -*ly* ending. Write the adjective forms of the adverbs above that can be changed.

   _____   _____   _____

BOOK 4

WORD PARTS

Use these word parts to complete the words in the sentences that follow.

bio- = life or living organisms
de- = completely, downward
dis- = reversal, negation, lack of
micro- = small
tele- = at a distance, far off

1. A _____ phone picks up voices far away.

2. The story of someone's life is a _____ graphy.

3. The device can detect _____ scopic levels of that chemical.

4. He became _____ couraged too easily.

5. We will _____ scend in the glass elevator.

PHRASAL VERBS AND OTHER IDIOMS

Reread the paragraphs these phrasal verbs are used in. The paragraph numbers are in parentheses. Then use the phrasal verbs to complete the sentences that follow.

based on (9)   spread around (27)
extended to (24)   take over (21)
involved in (3)

1. Her influence _____ many fields of science.

2. She was _____ some important projects.

3. People worried that insects would _____ the planet.

4. Her information was _____ scientific research.

5. He _____ the good news about her book.

ATTRACTIONS *Teacher's Guide*
© 1994 Contemporary Books
A Reproducible Exercise Page

DR. KING'S DREAM

(PAGES 17–29)

Pre-Reading Activities

Discussion Questions

1. About Georgia: Where is Georgia? What do you think the climate is like there? What do you know about the state? What is it well known for?

2. About Atlanta: (The Center for Nonviolent Social Change is a peace museum.) What would you find inside a peace museum?

3. About the civil rights movement: What do you know about the civil rights movement? Have you seen any television shows or movies on the subject? Have you read any books or heard any songs on the subject?

4. About Martin Luther King Jr.: What do you know about Martin Luther King Jr.? Have you seen pictures of him? What did he look like? What were some of his accomplishments?

5. About the title: What was Dr. King's dream? What is meant here by a *dream*?

6. About civil rights leaders: Do you know of any other civil rights leaders? What do you know about them?

7. About the photographs: What impression do you get of King and the civil rights movement from the photographs?

8. About the teaser: How could Martin Luther King Jr. have been identified by the wrong name on his birth certificate? (The answer is in the Sidelights. Martin was mistakenly identified as Michael because of his father's nickname. It was recorded on the birth certificate instead of Martin.)

Section Headings

"Sweet Auburn": Ask the students if they think this is the name of a place or a thing. When they read the section, they'll find it refers to King's birthplace. Ask them what color auburn is.

"The Early Years": This section is about King's childhood. Ask students what they know of his childhood before they read the text. After they read it, ask if their childhoods were similar or different and how.

"Freedom Riders": Ask students what they imagine freedom riders to be. Ask if they have ever participated in a political protest.

"A Prize for Peace": Ask students the following: What is the Nobel Peace Prize? Who has gotten it lately?

"A Prophecy Fulfilled": This section deals with King's tragic death as well as his legacy. Ask students if all prophecies are good ones.

"Memories of the Movement": Ask students what they expect to learn. Have them list what the museum contains after they read the section.

Important Vocabulary from the Reading

1. Discuss the vocabulary of the civil rights movement: *nonviolence, sit-ins, boycott, freedom riders, protest, social change, Jim Crow laws,* and *segregation.*

2. Have students find the meanings of the following terms, which may be new to them: *laser sculpture, arsonist, unconstitutional.*

3. Discuss the difference in meaning between *sadness* and *despair.*

4. King said, "I have a dream." What are some synonyms for *dream* in this context?

Activities to Accompany the Reading

Playing Word Games

Divide the class in half. Have half the class look for words that describe people or groups of people performing constructive acts (*leader, minister,* etc.). Have the other half look for words that describe people or groups of people performing destructive acts (*arsonist, mob,* etc.).

Improvising Scenes

1. Provide the class with a text of King's "I Have a Dream" speech. Have students take turns delivering parts of it.

2. Have someone role-play Coretta King calling King to tell him that he's won the Nobel Prize.

3. Have a student play Rosa Parks refusing to give up her seat on the bus to a white passenger.

4. Have a group of students role-play participating in a sit-in. Have them decide where, when, and why they are protesting.

Comparing and Contrasting

Have students reread the sections headed "Sweet Auburn" and "Memories of the Movement." Have them contrast the Center for Nonviolent Social Change with the National Civil Rights Museum.

Using Maps

On a map of the United States, have students find all the cities that are mentioned in the reading. Ask them the following: How far is Atlanta from Memphis? How far is Atlanta from Montgomery?

Summarizing Chronology

Have students prepare a time line of the life of King from the information provided in the chapter.

Discussion, Writing, or Research Topics

1. Have students research people from African-American history and people important to the civil rights movement. Some names to recommend include Harriet Tubman, Frederick Douglass, Rosa Parks, Coretta Scott King, Mohandas Gandhi, Henry David Thoreau, Ralph David Abernathy, Malcolm X, Andrew Young, and Jesse Jackson.

2. Students may research events and organizations from the civil rights movement's history. Some suggested topics include: *Brown v. Board of Education*, Southern Christian Leadership Conference (SCLC), Dexter Avenue Baptist Church, freedom rides, Montgomery to Selma march, King's assassination.

3. Give students copies of texts relating to the civil rights movement including King's "I Have a Dream" speech, his letter from jail, and his Nobel Prize acceptance speech. Students may also be given the lyrics of civil rights songs such as "Blowing in the Wind" and "Abraham, Martin, and John" or a copy of Dudley Randall's poem "Ballad of Birmingham" for discussion.

4. Have two teams of four students debate the following position: Nonviolence is the best means of promoting social change.

5. Discuss protest movements since King. Ask students the following: What other groups have organized to change their position or opportunities in society? What actions have they adopted from the civil rights movement?

Extension Activities

1. If there is a black history museum in your city, visit it as a group. If not, take a trip to a local library and make a list of all the books available on King.

2. Have the class listen to music of the civil rights movement.

3. Have a member of the National Association for the Advancement of Colored People (NAACP) or another civil rights organization visit your class for a lecture.

4. Have the class view the PBS documentary series, *Eyes on the Prize*, a look back at the civil rights movement of the 1960s.

5. Have the class view the film *The Long Walk Home*, a dramatization of the bus boycott.

For ESL Students

1. Ask students about the situation of civil rights in their countries. Ask if there have been any civil rights leaders. Ask whether or not someone from their country has won a Nobel Prize.

2. Ask students what they knew of Martin Luther King before reading the chapter and what they knew of the civil rights movement in the United States.

READING COMPREHENSION

A. Mark each of these statements *True* or *False*.

_____ **1.** Jim Crow laws allowed blacks and whites to mix freely in the South.

_____ **2.** The Center for Nonviolent Social Change is in Memphis.

_____ **3.** King read the writings of Mohandas Gandhi to learn about nonviolent protest.

_____ **4.** The Montgomery bus boycott was very successful.

_____ **5.** There are two different sculptures at the new Civil Rights Museum.

B. Reread each paragraph indicated. Then write a question you can answer with information from that paragraph. Then answer each question in a complete sentence.

1. Paragraph 3:

Question: _____

Answer: _____

2. Paragraph 20:

Question: _____

Answer: _____

3. Paragraph 25:

Question: _____

Answer: _____

4. Paragraph 31:

Question: _____

Answer: _____

READING COMPREHENSION (CONTINUED)

C. Circle the letter of the best answer to complete each sentence.

1. According to paragraph 9, in the North, blacks and whites (a) mixed more freely (b) practiced Jim Crow (c) all lived in Philadelphia.

2. The main idea of paragraph 15 is stated in (a) the first sentence (b) the second sentence (c) the last sentence.

3. According to paragraph 17, federal troops were used (a) to stop the freedom riders (b) to protect the freedom riders (c) to sing in King's church.

4. According to paragraph 22, King felt the Nobel Prize belonged (a) just to him (b) to his wife (c) to all people who want peace and justice.

5. According to paragraph 25, another interest of King's was (a) Chicago (b) economic opportunity (c) apartments.

D. Scan the reading and the Sidelights page to find the following information:

1. the year of King's birth: _____

2. King's age upon entering college: _____

3. the length of time of the Montgomery bus boycott: _____

4. how many miles King traveled in 1957: _____

5. how many Americans listened to the "I Have a Dream" speech: _____

6. King's age when he won the Nobel Prize: _____

7. the number of universities in Atlanta: _____

ATTRACTIONS *Teacher's Guide*
© 1994 Contemporary Books
A Reproducible Exercise Page

VOCABULARY PRACTICE

A. Use some of these words to complete the sentences that follow.

assassinated	inscription	prophecy	traditional
confront	integrated	racial	tragedy
crypts	legacy	sculpture	transportation
emotion	methods	stressed	voters

1. Some people are buried in graves, others in _____.

2. He made a _____ about his future, and it came true.

3. He worked hard to establish _____ equality.

4. It is a beautiful _____ of people working for civil rights.

5. They decided to boycott public _____.

6. People were shocked when King was _____.

B. Circle the word that best completes each sentence.

1. After King's death, people felt great sadness. In fact, they felt (despair, danger, devotion, power).

2. At home, King's parents stressed the importance of (television, preaching, discipline, theaters).

3. Forty (protesters, martyrs, convicts, ministers) to the cause of civil rights are listed on the beautiful fountain.

4. These are all nonviolent tactics except (sit-ins, boycotts, marches, arson).

5. The (restaurant, lounge, corridor, facade) of the Lorraine Hotel is part of the new Civil Rights Museum.

BOOK 4

WORDS IN CONTEXT

What does each word mean in the paragraph indicated? Reread the paragraphs. Then circle the letter of the correct answer.

1. <u>public facilities</u> (2): (a) restaurants, transportation, schools, and hotels (b) outside of buildings

2. <u>daily tasks</u> (4): (a) the usual activities one performs (b) special assignments

3. <u>pause for a moment</u> (6): (a) stop for a long time (b) stop for a short time

4. <u>bitter lessons</u> (9): (a) things that are hard to understand (b) things that are emotionally painful to understand

5. <u>segregated lunch counters</u> (15): (a) where blacks and whites ate together (b) where blacks and whites ate separately

6. <u>jeering crowds</u> (23): (a) people in favor of the activity of a group (b) people against the activity of a group

7. <u>economic opportunity</u> (25): (a) wealth (b) chance to earn money

8. <u>fatal bullet</u> (33): (a) bullet that killed (b) useless bullet

HOMONYMS, ANTONYMS, AND SIMILAR WORDS

Match each word in the column on the left with its opposite in the column on the right. Write the correct letters on the blank lines.

_____ 1. death   **(a)** segregation

_____ 2. integration   **(b)** war, upset, tumult

_____ 3. nonviolence   **(c)** birth

_____ 4. peace   **(d)** modest

_____ 5. stately   **(e)** experimental

_____ 6. traditional   **(f)** physical force

PATTERN PRACTICE

Connect these pairs of sentences with a comma and the word *but*.

1. He worked hard to change society. He was against violent methods.

_____

2. She had read Gandhi. She hadn't read Thoreau.

_____

3. They installed a new sculpture. Some people didn't like it.

_____

4. The boycott was effective. Some people ignored it.

_____

5. I would like to attend the Olympics. Tickets are hard to get.

_____

6. He wanted racial justice. He also wanted economic progress.

_____

PARTS OF SPEECH AND INFLECTED FORMS

Rewrite the noun phrases that follow using a past participle as an adjective. For help, reread the paragraphs indicated.

Example: documents someone wrote by hand (6) <u>handwritten copies</u>

1. a vision that becomes reality (5) _____

2. racially divided public transportation (14) _____

3. strong water-spraying devices (16) _____

4. individuals who feel grief (27) _____

5. efforts advanced by someone's devotion (34) _____

WORD PARTS

Study these word parts from the reading:

> *com-* = with, together
> *de-* = reversal or undoing
> *in-* = to cause to become
> *non-* = not
> *pro-* = onward or forward

Use the word parts above to complete the words in these sentences.

1. King practiced _____violence in all of his activities.

2. Martin _____tested doing dishes when he was a boy.

3. The _____scription on the crypt contains his own words.

4. In order for there to be _____segregation, protests would have to occur.

5. King's father worked in his church _____munity.

PHRASAL VERBS AND OTHER IDIOMS

Reread the paragraphs these idioms are used in. The paragraph numbers are in parentheses. Then use some of the idioms to complete the sentences that follow.

well-to-do (1)	Jim Crow (2)	painted a picture (19)
mixed freely (1)	up north (9)	checked into (21)

1. Segregation laws were also called _____ laws.

2. Philadelphia was a city _____.

3. In King's childhood community, all the neighbors _____.

4. In Memphis, where King was killed, the Lorraine Hotel was the place he had

_____.

ATTRACTIONS *Teacher's Guide*
© 1994 Contemporary Books
A Reproducible Exercise Page

THE HOUSE THAT WRIGHT BUILT

(PAGES 33–43)

Pre-Reading Activities

Discussion Questions

1. **About Frank Lloyd Wright:** What do you know about him? What was his occupation? Is he still living? Have you ever seen one of his buildings? Why do you think he became famous?

2. **About local architecture:** Can you describe the building you are in now? Is the style modern? What materials is it built of? Is it attractive? Is it accessible to the handicapped? Is it similar to the other buildings in the neighborhood, or are they older and a different architectural style? What is your favorite building in your city or town? Why do you like it? Are there any famous buildings in your area? Are they historical landmarks?

3. **About your dream house:** Where would you like to build your dream house? (Wright built his dream house in Wisconsin.) What would the exterior look like? How about the interior? What would you have on the grounds?

4. **About the title:** Where might you have seen a title like this before? (The title of this reading is a variation of the title of the well-known nursery rhyme "The House That Jack Built," an anonymous Mother Goose rhyme.)

5. **About the photographs accompanying this reading:** What do you notice about Wright's work from the photos in the text? What materials did he like to use? What generalizations can you make about his style?

6. **About the teaser:** Of all the buildings Wright designed in his lifetime, how many do you think are still standing? (The answer is in paragraph 24.)

Section Headings

"Shining Brow": This heading is the English translation of the Welsh word *Taliesin*, the name of Wright's famous Wisconsin home.

"The Chicago Years": For 20 years, Wright lived in Oak Park, Illinois, a suburb of Chicago. During this time, he designed many buildings in Oak Park and Chicago and became successful and prominent.

"Scandal": Some might call this period Wright's midlife crisis. It was a major turning point in his personal and professional life when he left his family in Oak Park to travel and then move to Wisconsin with another woman.

"Tragedy at Taliesin": Some moralists might have considered the tragedy punishment for the scandalous behavior of Wright and Cheney, but the tragedy went far beyond poetic justice and affected many innocent people. After completing the reading, students may want to discuss the following questions: Do people who are good, moral, and conventional enjoy better luck and greater happiness than those who are not? Also, would Wright's relationship with Cheney be considered scandalous today? Would it cost him most of his clients?

"Taliesin Today": Ask students to predict what information will be supplied in this section. Some good predictions would be information about the present condition of the house, who lives there now, who visits there now, and what is planned for the future of this famous place.

"What Wright Built": Students should expect a summary of Wright's major achievements— discussion of his most important structures and major architectural innovations.

Important Vocabulary from the Reading

1. Discuss the meanings of the following antonyms, one word in each pair of which is in the text: *Oriental / Occidental, horizontal / vertical,* and *hope / despair.*

2. Discuss the geological words *valley, waterfall, pond,* and *prairie.*

3. Discuss the meaning of *sophisticated.* Ask students if Wright was a sophisticated man. Ask them if a computer is a sophisticated machine. Have students check the origin of the word and the meaning of *soph-.* Have them discuss the meanings of *sophomore* and *sophistry.*

4. Discuss the word *picturesque*. What does the suffix *-esque* mean? (It means "like" or "in the style of.") Ask if students know any other words with that ending. (*Statuesque* is one.)

Activities to Accompany the Reading

Playing Word Games

After students complete the entire reading, write these sentences on the chalkboard. Have students complete the sentences with appropriate past-tense verbs. Students should not use the text for help.

1. Wright's mother _____ pictures of churches over his bed.

2. When he was a boy, Wright often _____ about building a house on his grandfather's land.

3. Before finishing college, Wright _____ school and _____ to Chicago.

4. Wright _____ Taliesin into the side of the hill.

5. The cook _____ a match and _____ it into the dining room.

6. The Imperial Hotel _____ its ground during the earthquake.

Improvising Scenes

1. Have pairs of students participate in interviews, with one student taking the role of the reporter and the other being Wright. Then have students share with the group some of the best questions and answers.

2. With pairs of students taking turns being the architect and the client, have each student describe his or her dream house. Then have each one write a paragraph about his or her partner's dream house.

Reading for Details

1. Have students scan the text for examples of innovative buildings that Wright built.

2. Have students scan the text for information about Wright's character and personality. List his good and bad points on the board.

Using Maps

On a map of the U.S.A., find and point out to the class the following places where Wright lived: Spring Green and Madison, Wisconsin; Chicago, Illinois; and Scottsdale, Arizona. Ask students why the school moves to Arizona in the winter. Ask students if they think Madison's climate is much different from Chicago's.

Discussion, Writing, or Research Topics

1. Often, people who have suffered a tragedy in a certain place want to leave that place and never return. Ask students why they think Wright wanted to stay at Taliesin.

2. After they read about Wright in an encyclopedia, biography, or autobiography, have each student select a favorite Wright design to write about. Each student should photocopy the structure and write a paragraph about it. The students' work might then be hung on a wall or combined in a book for display.

Extension Activities

1. If there are any Wright buildings in your area, take a class trip to visit them.

2. Have students read Greek legends, and have each student tell one to the class.

For ESL Students

Have students answer the following questions about the reading. Have them answer orally without consulting the text.

• How did Wright's mother help him become interested in architecture?
• What scandal was Wright involved in?
• What tragedy happened at Taliesin?
• What are some of the interesting features of Taliesin?
• How many wives did Wright have?
• What is the name of a famous building he designed?
• How old was Wright when he died?
• Who lives at Taliesin today?
• Where is Taliesin West?

READING COMPREHENSION

A. Mark each of these statements *True* or *False*.

_____ **1.** Wright wanted to build a house on top of the hill.

_____ **2.** The phoenix was an unusual bird that lived only in Greece.

_____ **3.** The cook started the first fire at Taliesin.

_____ **4.** All of Wright's buildings are in the prairie style.

_____ **5.** Wright believed that a building should fit in well with its environment.

B. Reread each paragraph indicated. Then write a question you can answer with information from that paragraph. Then answer each question with a complete sentence.

1. Paragraph 3:

Question: _____

Answer: _____

2. Paragraph 12:

Question: _____

Answer: _____

3. Paragraph 19:

Question: _____

Answer: _____

4. Paragraph 26:

Question: _____

Answer: _____

5. Paragraph 29:

Question: _____

Answer: _____

READING COMPREHENSION (CONTINUED)

C. Scan the reading to find the answers to these questions. Write one- or two-word answers.

1. In what year was Wright born? _____

2. What state is Taliesin in? _____

3. What city is it near? _____

4. Who taught Wright that form should follow function? _____

5. How many major fires were there at Taliesin? _____

6. How many times did Wright marry? _____

7. When did the Wrights open their school at Taliesin? _____

8. What city and state is Taliesin West in? _____

D. Reread paragraphs 8, 12, 20, 27, and 29. Look for information about Wright's architectural style. List four things he liked.

_____   _____

_____   _____

E. Reread paragraphs 5 and 29. Write two sentences about things he didn't like.

_____

_____

F. Reread paragraph 23. List two unusual features of the Frank Lloyd Wright School of Architecture.

_____

_____

ATTRACTIONS *Teacher's Guide*
© 1994 Contemporary Books
A Reproducible Exercise Page

VOCABULARY PRACTICE

A. Use some of these words to complete the sentences that follow.

architect   environment   generation   quarry
clients   fabrics   innovative   scandal
concrete   facility   patio   sophisticated
despair   faculty   prairie   textures

1. Wright was an _____ architect. He liked to try new things, to do what hadn't been done before.

2. Wright fell in love with the wife of one of his _____.

3. When she was murdered, Wright felt great _____.

4. Wright's second wife was a _____ and artistic woman.

5. Wright's third wife was much younger than he. In fact, she came from a different _____.

6. Wright designed not only buildings but also furniture, glassware, and _____.

7. When he designed a room, he liked to use a variety of _____, some rough and some smooth.

8. Wright's buildings were always appropriate for their _____.

B. Circle the word that doesn't belong in each group.

1. an occupation: architect, draftsman, client, carpenter

2. part of a building: ceiling, skylight, ramp, scandal

3. a building material: wood, stone, quarry, glass

4. a natural part of the landscape: river, patio, valley, prairie

BOOK 4

WORDS IN CONTEXT

What does each word mean in the paragraph indicated? Reread the paragraphs. Then circle the letter of the correct answer.

1. <u>legend</u> (1): (a) a true story (b) a story told from one generation to another that can't be verified

2. <u>horizontal</u> (8): (a) sideways (b) up and down

3. <u>vision</u> (9): (a) eyesight (b) an idea about a future accomplishment

4. <u>scandal</u> (10): (a) an exciting event that everyone looks forward to (b) an action talked about and considered immoral

5. <u>spacious</u> (12): (a) roomy (b) crowded

6. <u>fired</u> (14): (a) burned (b) dismissed from a job

7. <u>overwhelming</u> (16): (a) ending (b) more than the person can handle

8. <u>bridging</u> (17): (a) bringing together, connecting (b) walking across a bridge

9. <u>level</u> (27): (a) steady and reliable (b) flat, even, exactly horizontal

10. <u>generation</u> (29): (a) about 10 years (b) about 30 years

HOMONYMS, SYNONYMS, AND SIMILAR WORDS

Match each word in the column on the right with the correct word or phrase in the column on the left. Write the correct letters on the blank lines.

_____ 1. apparent   **(a)** scenic

_____ 2. environment   **(b)** wordly, experienced

_____ 3. function   **(c)** can be seen

_____ 4. landscape   **(d)** use

_____ 5. picturesque   **(e)** surroundings

_____ 6. sophisticated   **(f)** scenery

ATTRACTIONS *Teacher's Guide*
© 1994 Contemporary Books
A Reproducible Exercise Page

PATTERN PRACTICE

Study these sentences from paragraph 16.

Purpose or Reason	Action
To erase painful memories,	he made changes in the house.
To finance this remodeling,	he accepted new projects.

Now complete the following sentences with information from the paragraphs indicated.

1. To please his wife Oglivanna, _____
_____. (19)

2. To bring the outdoor scenery indoors, _____
_____. (20)

3. To allow students to work outdoors year-round, _____
_____. (23)

PARTS OF SPEECH AND INFLECTED FORMS

The word *building* can be a noun, verb, or adjective. After each of these sentences, write which part of speech it is.

1. Someone is *building* a house next door to us. _____

2. Children usually enjoy playing with *building* blocks. _____

3. That *building* was built by Frank Lloyd Wright. _____

4. *Building* a house is hard work. _____

5. He thought about *building* a house. _____

6. Are you *building* a fence around your house? _____

ATTRACTIONS *Teacher's Guide*
© 1994 Contemporary Books
A Reproducible Exercise Page

BOOK 4

WORD PARTS

Study the meanings of these word parts from the reading:

sym- = with, together, at the same time
uni- = only one
in- and *un-* = not
-pathy = feeling, suffering, disease

Now answer these questions in complete sentences.

1. Who is nicer—a sympathetic or an unsympathetic person?

_____

2. When should you express your sympathy to someone?

_____

3. What is a unique idea?

_____

PHRASAL VERBS AND OTHER IDIOMS

Reread the paragraphs that the idioms in the column on the left are used in. Then match each idiom with its definition in the column on the right. Write the correct letters on the blank lines.

_____ **1.** get along with (13)

_____ **2.** get rid of (29)

_____ **3.** look like (2)

_____ **4.** receive word (15)

_____ **5.** stand for (17)

_____ **6.** waiting list (23)

(a) resemble

(b) symbolize

(c) dispose of something undesirable

(d) have a friendly relationship with

(e) names of people wanting to get into something

(f) get information about some event

ATTRACTIONS *Teacher's Guide*
© 1994 Contemporary Books
A Reproducible Exercise Page

WIZARD AT WORK

(PAGES 47–57)

Pre-Reading Activities

Discussion Questions

1. About Thomas Edison: What are Edison's most famous inventions? What do you know about his childhood? About his adult life?

2. About inventions: What were some of the most important inventions of the 19th century? What about the 20th century? What's the difference between an invention and a discovery?

3. About the phonograph: How has the phonograph been improved since Edison's time? What changes have made reproduced sound more lifelike?

4. About curiosity: When is it a good quality? When is it inappropriate or dangerous? Is it always easy to tell when curiosity is leading someone into trouble?

5. About the title: What does the word *wizard* mean to you? What kind of a wizard do you think Edison was?

6. About the photographs accompanying the reading: What Edison inventions are in the pictures? Are they all still used today? Do they look the same?

7. About the teaser: What were the first words Edison recorded? (The answer is in paragraph 15.)

Section Headings

"Bright Ideas": Define a pun. Then discuss the pun in this heading.

"A Curious Boy": Discuss the two meanings of the word *curious*. One is having curiosity. The other is being the object of other people's curiosity. After students have read the section, ask them which meaning is intended here. Both could be considered relevant. Edison was curious in both ways.

"Early Inventions": Point out that in this heading, *early* means in the first part of Edison's career. Have students scan the reading and then list some of these early inventions.

"Sound and Light": Ask students what scientific field is concerned with the nature of sound and light. (physics) Ask them what else physicists study. (electricity, etc.) Point out that Edison's major interests related to the field of physics but extended to other areas, such as chemistry.

"The Invention Factory": Ask students to guess why Edison's West Orange facility was called an invention factory. When they read the section, they will learn that Edison not only produced inventions but also manufactured them at this facility.

Important Vocabulary from the Reading

1. Compare and contrast the words *curious* and *inquisitive.*

2. Have students change the verb *invent* into two nouns (*invention* and *inventor*) and an adjective (*inventive*).

3. Discuss two meanings of the word *conductor*: one related to trains; the other, to electricity.

4. Discuss the scientific terms *generator, sound waves, filament,* and *vacuum.*

Activities to Accompany the Reading

Playing Word Games

Write the words listed below on the chalkboard. Discuss the similarities and/or differences between words in each group. Then write sentences 1–7 on the board, and have students use some of the words to complete them.

extraordinary / strange
quality / quantity
make / create / manufacture
explore / research / experiment

1. Before she wrote the essay about Edison, she did a lot of _____ in the library.

2. Edison had to _____ with a lot of different filaments before he made a practical, long-lasting light bulb.

3. When you _____ products, you make many copies of the same item in a factory.

4. You can _____ a place by going there and looking around very carefully.

5. High _____ means "judged to be very good."

6. A large _____ means a large amount.

7. An _____ person is a person who is outstanding in some way.

Improvising Scenes

1. Have students pretend they are Edison and the conductor who threw him off the train. (paragraph 9)

2. Have students act out the scene involving Edison and his boss. (paragraph 13)

Reading for Specific Information

1. Have students reread paragraph 13. Ask them what they can infer about Edison from the behavior described here. Ask them what sort of a person he was. Have them choose adjectives that describe a person who behaves this way.

2. Have students reread paragraphs 16 and 17. Ask them what various pieces of equipment were needed in order to sell electricity to the general public.

3. Ask students what two places they would visit to learn more about Edison's life and work. According to the reading, West Orange, New Jersey, and Dearborn, Michigan, are the major Edison sites.

Using Maps

On a map of North America, locate all the places mentioned in the reading as sites associated with Edison. These are Ohio, Kentucky, Canada, New Jersey, New York, and Michigan. Ask the class the significance of each of these places in terms of Edison's life and work.

Discussion, Writing, or Research Topics

Have students consider these questions in a class discussion or short essay:

- What would your life be like without electricity? What would you miss most?
- What do you think Edison would be working on today if he were still alive?

Extension Activities

Have students read more about Edison, either in an encyclopedia or a biography. They should take notes, then come to class prepared to tell an interesting fact or anecdote about Edison's inventions and/or his personal life.

For ESL Students

1. Bring a lamp or a picture of one to class. Ask students to find these parts: the bulb, socket, electric cord, and plug. Ask them what two things must be done to make the light go on.

2. Discuss what a nursery rhyme is, and have students read a few aloud, including "Mary Had a Little Lamb." Ask them if there are similar short poems for children in their native languages. If so, have the students each translate one as a homework assignment and then recite it in class.

3. Have students practice pronunciation.

   - Have them say these words that contain the letters *ch*, pronounced *k*:

     chemicals   mechanic
     chemistry   technological

   - Have them say these words that contain the letter *x*, pronounced *ks*:

     explore   extraordinary

   - Have them say these words that contain the sound *f* made with *f*, *ff*, *ph*, and *gh*.

     artificial   office   phonograph   enough
     facility   offer   telegraph   laugh

4. Explain that the letter *c* has two sounds: *k* and *s*. It is usually pronounced *s* when it comes before the letter *e*, *i*, or *y*, and it is usually pronounced *k* when it comes before other letters. Write these words on the board, and say them aloud.

   accidentally   create   electric
   concentrate   device   replica

READING COMPREHENSION

A. Mark each of these statements *True* or *False*.

_____ **1.** Edison began to do experiments when he was a boy.

_____ **2.** Edison lived in New Jersey all his life.

_____ **3.** Edison's company invented and manufactured machines.

_____ **4.** Edison sometimes improved other people's inventions.

_____ **5.** Although Edison became famous, he never made much money.

B. Answer these questions in complete sentences.

1. Why did Edison want to make money from his inventions?

_____

2. In your opinion, which of Edison's inventions changed the world the most?

_____

_____

3. Why was Edison so successful? Give three reasons.

_____

_____

_____

4. Why did Edison's West Orange facility have both laboratories and factories?

_____

5. Why did a Japanese tourist bow to Edison's lab coat?

_____

6. What does the quotation in paragraph 25 mean?

_____

7. According to paragraph 26, what was Edison's research style?

_____

READING COMPREHENSION (CONTINUED)

C. Scan the reading for eight of Edison's inventions. Write them below.

_____   _____   _____   _____

_____   _____   _____   _____

D. Scan the reading for three accidents that Edison had. Write a sentence about each.

_____

_____

_____

E. Circle the letter of the best answer to complete each sentence.

1. Edison probably didn't complain about his deafness because (a) the silence helped him to think without interruption (b) he didn't want people to feel sorry for him (c) he couldn't talk to people after he became deaf.

2. Edison hired chemists and mechanics to work for him because (a) he was lazy (b) he needed their ideas for things to invent (c) he needed help in researching all the ideas he had.

3. The phonograph was Edison's favorite invention because (a) he couldn't hear it (b) it worked the first time he tried it (c) it was the most original of his inventions.

4. Edison believed that great discoveries came mostly from (a) genius (b) hard work (c) mathematical analysis.

5. Edison believed that he could create useful inventions. He had (a) self-confidence (b) a desire to be inquisitive (c) a love of fires.

6. According to the Sidelights page, New Jersey (a) has more residents than any other state (b) is mostly urban and industrial (c) has more people per square mile than any other state.

VOCABULARY PRACTICE

Use some of these words to complete the sentences that follow.

baggage	customers	manufactured	phonograph
battery	facility	nickname	research
bulb	genius	offered	silent
concentrate	improved	patent	telegraph

1. When the government gives an inventor a _____ on a particular invention, the inventor then controls the manufacture and sale of the invention.

2. Edison didn't invent the electric light _____, but he made the first long-lasting one.

3. Edison's _____, the Wizard of Menlo Park, suggests that people considered his inventions as amazing as magic.

4. A _____ is a source of electrical energy.

5. Edison's factories _____ many products.

6. _____ movies didn't have any sound.

7. Most people agree that Edison was a _____.

8. In 1869, Edison's boss _____ to buy his patents for improvements on the stock ticker.

9. Edison's hearing loss helped him to _____ on his work because he couldn't hear conversation or noise around him.

10. Edison _____ Alexander Graham Bell's telephone so that people didn't have to shout into it anymore.

11. The _____ was Edison's favorite of all his inventions.

12. Edison did a lot of _____ by trial and error.

WORDS IN CONTEXT

What does each word mean in the paragraph indicated? Reread the paragraphs. Then circle the letter of each correct answer.

1. <u>record</u> (1): (a) a disk to play on a phonograph (b) the greatest quantity of something

2. <u>curiosity</u> (6): (a) wanting to know (b) something strange

3. <u>annoying</u> (7): (a) interesting (b) bothersome

4. <u>conclusions</u> (8): (a) directions (b) statements of what the experiment proved

5. <u>conductor</u> (9): (a) the employee in charge of passengers on a train (b) something that carries electricity

6. <u>last</u> (16): (a) continue to burn (b) stop burning

7. <u>insights</u> (24): (a) understanding (b) the ability to look at something

8. <u>perspiration</u> (25): (a) hard work (b) moisture from the human body

HOMONYMS, SYNONYMS, AND SIMILAR WORDS

Match each word in the column on the left with the correct word or phrase in the column on the right. Write the correct letters on the blank lines.

_____ 1. concentrate

_____ 2. curious

_____ 3. exaggerate

_____ 4. filament

_____ 5. generate

_____ 6. obtain

_____ 7. prediction

_____ 8. vacuum

(a) a thread-like wire

(b) produce or transform energy

(c) inquisitive

(d) get

(e) overstate the truth

(f) a completely empty space

(g) think hard about something

(h) a guess about the future

ATTRACTIONS *Teacher's Guide*
© 1994 Contemporary Books
A Reproducible Exercise Page

PATTERN PRACTICE

Study these irregular adjective forms:

Base Form	Comparative Form	Superlative Form
good	better	best
bad	worse	worst

Now use some of the words above to complete these sentences.

1. My life is _____ than my sister's. (Mine is not as good as hers.)

2. She always has good luck. Her luck is much _____ than mine.

3. Yesterday, for example, everything went wrong for me. It was the _____ day of my life.

4. First, I felt _____ because I overslept. I knew I'd be late for work.

5. Then I felt even _____ when I burned my toast and spilled hot coffee all over my new jacket.

6. The _____ thing about yesterday was that it finally ended.

7. I hope tomorrow will be a _____ day for me.

PARTS OF SPEECH AND INFLECTED FORMS

Circle the word that best completes each sentence.

1. Thomas Alva Edison was a great (invention, invented, inventor).

2. Edison made some (improves, improvements, improved) in Bell's telephone.

3. Did Edison (invent, invented, inventor) the movie camera?

4. Edison's hearing loss helped his (concentrate, concentration, concentrated).

5. Edison (created, creation, create) many useful inventions.

6. In school, Edison (annoying, annoyed, annoys) his teacher.

WORD PARTS

Study the meanings of these word parts. Then use some of them to complete the sentences that follow.

extra- = outside, beyond, more than
-graph = that which writes or draws
kine- = movement, motion

phon-, *phono-* = voice, sound
-scope = an instrument for looking at something
tele- = far, distant

1. A micro_____ is used for looking at very small things.

2. _____ics is the science of sound.

3. A phono_____ record has grooves that can reproduce sounds.

4. An _____ordinary person has unusual abilities.

5. A _____graph machine sends messages far away.

PHRASAL VERBS AND OTHER IDIOMS

Reread the paragraphs that these idioms are used in. The paragraph numbers are in parentheses. Then use some of the idioms to complete the sentences that follow. Some sentences need past-tense verbs.

find out (6)   run over (15)   dream up (25)
burn down (6)   play back (15)   trial and error (26)
big break (13)   catch on (22)

1. My brother was only five years old when we _____ that he was a musical genius.

2. But he didn't learn to play the piano by _____. He took lessons and studied hard for many years.

3. He got his first _____ when he won a music contest.

4. Lately, his musical style has _____ with audiences.

5. His fans love the melodies he _____ in his head.

ATTRACTIONS *Teacher's Guide*
© 1994 Contemporary Books
A Reproducible Exercise Page

THE WRIGHT FLIGHT
(PAGES 61–71)

Pre-Reading Activities
Discussion Questions

1. About the Wright brothers: What were their first names? What did they invent?

2. About modern transportation: Which came first: the steamship, train, automobile, or airplane? Can you list these forms of transportation in the order they were invented? In what year was each introduced?

3. About airplanes: Who has flown in an airplane? Do you know how fast and how high commercial planes fly today? What is a jet plane? What is supersonic flight? What does the word *aviation* mean? Guess what the Latin word *avis* means.

4. About alternate forms of flying: How else can people fly besides using an airplane? Have any of you ever gone gliding or hot-air ballooning? Do you want to? Do you think these sports are dangerous?

5. About hobbies: Do you have a hobby that could someday become your vocation? What is it?

6. About the chapter title: What is the pun in the title "The Wright Flight"?

7. About the photographs accompanying the reading: What do they show about early aviation? How is modern aviation different?

8. About the teaser: How long do you think Orville Wright's first flight lasted? (The answer is in paragraph 18. The famous photograph of that first flight is on the cover of the book.)

Section Headings

"A Dream of Flying": Ask students if they think this heading refers to a dream during sleep or to a goal. They may scan the section for the answer.

"Balloons and Gliders": Ask students how these two items are related. Both are for flying. Ask students which they think was invented first.

"Trying and Trying Again": Ask students what this heading says about the Wright brothers. Encourage students to come up with appropriate nouns for what the brothers had, such as *perseverance, persistence, determination.*

"A 12-Second Flight": Ask students if they were surprised at how short the first flight was.

"Troubles and Tributes": Ask students if the two nouns in this subhead are synonyms or antonyms. Ask for examples of tributes. Compare this phrase to "trials and tribulations."

Important Vocabulary from the Reading

1. Bring models of a few different airplanes to class, and have students name the parts. Important words about airplanes include *propeller, engine, wing, controls, tail,* and *aviation.*

2. Discuss the similarities and differences between word pairs *desert* and *sand, determined* and *stubborn, motor* and *engine, glider* and *airplane.* Also discuss *hobby, avocation,* and *vocation;* and the difference between an airplane with propellers and a jet.

3. Point out that *sound* in this reading is a geographical term (see paragraph 11).

Activities to Accompany the Reading
Playing Word Games

Give students three minutes to write three adjectives to describe each of the people or things listed below. Allow them to use the text or to work in teams.

- Wilbur Wright
- Orville Wright
- Kitty Hawk
- the *Flyer*
- the first successful airplane flight
- Kill Devil Hills today

Improvising Scenes

1. Have students pretend that they are at Kill Devil Hills on December 17, 1903. Have them improvise their dialogue immediately before and immediately after that first takeoff.

2. Have students imagine that they are going to fly the *Flyer*. Orville Wright is giving them some last-minute instructions and warnings. Have them improvise the conversation.

Using Maps

Have students find Dayton, Ohio, and Kitty Hawk, North Carolina, on a map of the United States. Ask them how the brothers probably got from one place to the other. (They traveled by train and boat.)

Discussion, Writing, or Research Topics

1. Have students make a list of inventions other than the airplane that have changed the world. Have each student choose one inventor and invention to read about in an encyclopedia or biography. Then have each give a brief oral report or write a paragraph about their inventor and invention.

2. Have students research one of the famous people in the history of aviation and tell or write about him or her. Some people to include in a list of choices are Charles Voisin and Gabriel Voisin, Glenn H. Curtiss, Donald Douglas, Amelia Earhart, Charles Lindbergh, Howard Hughes, Bessie Coleman, and Chuck Yeager. American astronauts might also be included.

3. Have students tell or write a narrative essay about their most exciting or scary experience flying or traveling some other way.

Extension Activities

1. Show a videotape about aviation.

2. Have each student plan an airplane trip to a place he or she would like to visit. The assignment includes finding the cost of a round-trip ticket, the types of flights (nonstop or with stops) available, the number of miles that would be covered, the type of airplane, and the estimated travel time. Students may also compare the various airlines and categories of passenger seating and service (coach, business, first class, etc.) and choose the best way to go in terms of time, money, and comfort.

For ESL Students

1. Be sure that students understand the coin toss and know which side is heads and which is tails on a coin.

2. Point out the two opposites of the word *light*: *dark* and *heavy*.

3. It's easy for ESL students to confuse these words: *accept, except, expect.* Review their meanings.

4. A. Ask students what rules they know about silent letters in English. Then review the following rules, which relate to words in the reading.

   - When the letters *gn* are in the same syllable, the *g* is silent.
   - When the letters *wr* are in the same syllable, the *w* is silent.
   - The letters *gh* are either silent or pronounced *f*.
   - When *sc* is followed by *e, i,* or *y,* the *c* is silent. Examples include *scissors, science,* and *scene.*
   - When the letters *ui* are together, the *u* is often silent.
   - When a word ends with *mb,* the *b* is silent.

   B. Write the words listed on the chalkboard. Ask students to name the silent letter or letters in each word. Then read the words aloud.

built	flight	wreck
climb	higher	Wright
design	right	write
fascinating	sign	wrong

READING COMPREHENSION

A. Mark each of these statements *True* or *False*.

_____ **1.** The older Wright brother died first.

_____ **2.** Kitty Hawk is on the West Coast of the United States.

_____ **3.** The Wright brothers were successful partly because they didn't give up easily.

_____ **4.** Photography was one of Orville Wright's hobbies.

_____ **5.** The United States government was eager to buy the Wright brothers' invention.

_____ **6.** The buildings that Orville Wright and Wilbur Wright built are still standing in Kill Devil Hills.

B. Answer the following questions in complete sentences.

1. Why did the Wright brothers choose Kitty Hawk for their experiments? What three advantages did the site have?

_____

_____

_____

2. How did people fly before airplanes were invented? Name two ways.

_____

3. What evidence shows that the Wright brothers didn't take unnecessary risks with their lives?

_____

4. Why were the Wright brothers successful in developing controlled flight? Give two reasons.

_____

_____

READING COMPREHENSION (CONTINUED)

C. Paraphrase these statements. (Write the ideas in your own words.) For help, reread the paragraphs indicated.

1. They kept costs to a minimum. (10)

   _____

2. This land is almost completely surrounded by water. (11)

   _____

3. It didn't have the lifting power they expected. (14)

   _____

4. Their achievement was "very modest compared with that of the birds." (19)

   _____

5. They were turned down. (22)

   _____

6. Some visitors get hooked on flight. (26)

   _____

D. Using information from the reading and your general knowledge about inventions, write _B_ before the items that were invented before the airplane and _A_ before those invented after the airplane.

_____ 1. automobile   _____ 6. radio

_____ 2. bicycle   _____ 7. sewing machine

_____ 3. camera   _____ 8. telegraph machine

_____ 4. electricity   _____ 9. television

_____ 5. glider   _____ 10. train

ATTRACTIONS *Teacher's Guide*
© 1994 Contemporary Books
A Reproducible Exercise Page

NAME _____

VOCABULARY PRACTICE

A. Use some of these words to complete the sentences that follow.

airplane	engine	kite	reproduction
aviation	experiments	operate	steer
balloon	glider	pilot	tail
control	hangar	pioneers	transportation
design	invention	propeller	wings

1. Four words that name parts of an airplane are _____,
_____, _____, and _____.

2. Four words that name things that can fly are _____,
_____, _____, and _____.

3. A person who operates a plane is a _____.

4. The Wright brothers were _____ in the field of aviation.

5. That airplane is not the original. It's a _____.

6. He tried to turn the plane, but he couldn't do it. He lost _____ of the plane.

7. The Wright brothers did many _____ with gliders.

8. Then they changed the _____ of their gliders.

B. Circle the word that best completes each sentence.

1. The wind (affects, afflicts, effects, expects) how a glider will fly.

2. The brothers didn't (accept, affect, expect, invent) any money from others.

3. A (legal, limited, lose, loose) wire caused Orville Wright's airplane accident.

4. The Wright brothers considered birds the (extras, experts, engines, pilots) on the aerodynamics of flying.

5. The brothers had a lot of (financial, musical, mechanical, artistic) ability.

BOOK 4

WORDS IN CONTEXT

What does each phrase mean in the paragraph indicated? Reread the paragraphs. Then circle the letter of the correct answer.

1. <u>sand dune</u> (3): (a) a flat, sandy area (b) a hill of sand

2. <u>spare time</u> (5): (a) leisure time, free time (b) time to use sparingly

3. <u>brilliant</u> (5): (a) very intelligent (b) shining very brightly

4. <u>aerodynamics</u> (8): (a) a fast airplane (b) principles about the effects of air in motion

5. <u>cautious</u> (9): (a) willing to risk death or injury (b) careful to avoid danger

6. <u>zoom</u> (27): (a) travel very fast (b) glide on air currents

HOMONYMS, SYNONYMS, AND SIMILAR WORDS

Check the meanings of these homonyms in a dictionary. Then use some of them to complete the sentences that follow.

accept / except   affect / effect
hangar / hanger   right / write / Wright

1. I didn't _____ his job offer. I turned it down.

2. Did I do the _____ thing or the wrong thing?

3. Did the Wright brothers ever _____ a book about their experiments?

4. When they're not being used, a coat is hung on a _____ and an airplane is kept in a _____ .

5. The invention of the airplane has had a great _____ on world travel.

6. Everyone in my family loves to fly _____ me. I'm afraid of flying.

7. The Wright brothers had no idea of how their invention would _____ the travel industry.

ATTRACTIONS *Teacher's Guide*
© 1994 Contemporary Books
A Reproducible Exercise Page

PATTERN PRACTICE

After the word *suggest*, you may use a gerund (a verbal noun ending with *-ing*) or some other noun.

Examples: Orville suggested a movable tail.
Wilbur suggested linking the wing and tail mechanisms to one control.

After *suggest*, you may also use *that* plus a subject and base verb form.

Example: Chanute suggested that Wilbur choose a site near an ocean.

Complete these sentences following each of the patterns above.

1. My friends suggested _____.

2. My relatives have often suggested _____.

3. The salesperson suggested _____.

PARTS OF SPEECH AND INFLECTED FORMS

A. Complete each sentence with an irregular past-tense verb.

1. The Wright brothers _____ and _____ bicycles.

2. The Wright brothers _____ the first airplane.

3. The brothers _____ Ohio and _____ to North Carolina to do experiments with gliders.

4. The 1901 glider didn't always work right. Sometimes it _____ sideways in the air and then _____ to the ground.

B. The words *design*, *experiment*, and *control* can be nouns or verbs. Use these words in these sentences. Add plural noun endings or past-tense verb endings where necessary.

1. Orville and Wilbur _____ with gliders for four years.

2. Many times, their _____ were disappointing.

3. The Wright brothers _____ a lightweight engine for the *Flyer*.

4. Orville _____ the plane by moving his body from side to side.

BOOK 4

WORD PARTS

Study the meanings of these word parts from the reading.

aero- = air, of the air, connected with flying   *bi-* = two
re- = again   *un-* and *dis-* = not

Use the word parts above to complete the words in these sentences.

1. The United States government _____produced the *Flyer*.

2. A _____production of the *Flyer* is now at Kill Devil Hills.

3. A _____plane has two main wing surfaces, one above the other.

4. Failure is usually _____couraging, but it didn't make the Wright brothers give up.

5. When Orville Wright and Wilbur Wright changed the design of their glider, they _____designed it.

6. It is _____usual for two brothers to work together so well.

7. Pilots must understand _____dynamics.

PHRASAL VERBS AND OTHER IDIOMS

Reread the paragraphs that the idioms in the column on the left are used in. Then match each idiom with its definition in the column on the right. Write the correct letters on the blank lines.

_____ 1. find out (3)   **(a)** refuse an offer

_____ 2. get hooked on (26)   **(b)** alternate; first one, then another

_____ 3. lift off (16), take off (27)   **(c)** want to do something often

_____ 4. take turns (19)   **(d)** leave the ground, begin to fly

_____ 5. turn down (22)   **(e)** get information about, learn about

ATTRACTIONS *Teacher's Guide*
© 1994 Contemporary Books
A Reproducible Exercise Page

A DIFFERENT DRUMMER

(PAGES 75–85)

Pre-Reading Activities

Discussion Questions

1. About Thoreau: Who was he? When did he live? What was unconventional about his behavior? Why is he famous?

2. About Walden Pond: Where is it—what state and what section of the country? Have you read about the fund-raising efforts to preserve it as a natural environment? Do you think it's important to save one small area just because it once inspired a famous literary work?

3. About conservation: What are the concerns of conservationists today? What are they trying to do to protect the environment?

4. About a love of nature: Do you enjoy beautiful, natural places? Do you enjoy hiking or camping outdoors or visiting national parks? Why do you enjoy these activities? How do they make you feel?

5. About a philosophy of life: Thoreau had very specific ideas about how people should live to achieve happiness. What is your philosophy of life? What are some examples of moral and immoral behavior in your judgment?

6. About the chapter title: The phrase "a different drummer" is quoted from Thoreau's most famous work, *Walden*. What do you think the quotation at the end of the reading means?

7. About the photographs accompanying the reading: What do these reveal about Thoreau and about Walden Pond?

8. About the teaser: Why would Thoreau have had a library of 700 books all written by himself? (The answer is in paragraph 22.)

Section Headings

"The Simple Life": Ask students if this heading refers to an easy life or a life that is uncluttered, uncomplicated, reduced to basic needs and important endeavors. After students finish the reading, have them go back and define the term *simple life*.

"Before Walden Pond": Ask students what information they expect to find here, The emphasis is on biographical facts that explain why Thoreau made the unusual decision to live alone in a one-room cabin in a forest.

"The Necessities of Life": Students may discuss what these necessities are. Of course, they include what is needed to keep a person alive. But ask students if the term shouldn't also include what is needed to make a person want to live, to help a person find meaning and purpose in life. Ask students to think about what Thoreau needed to make his life meaningful.

"The Seasons at Walden Pond": At Walden, Thoreau enjoyed the four seasons that Americans are so familiar with. Remind students that in some parts of the world, there are only two seasons, rainy and dry. Ask students who have visited or lived in other countries how many seasons there are in those countries.

"Important Works": Define for students *fiction* and *nonfiction*. Ask them if Thoreau wrote fiction or nonfiction. Ask them what makes a literary work important. Thoreau's work has been important because it has influenced what people believe and how they behave.

"Remembering Thoreau": Ask students if they knew anything about Thoreau prior to being introduced to this reading. Note that he is remembered not only for his own writings but for the influence he had on other writers and world leaders, such as Gandhi and Martin Luther King Jr.

Important Vocabulary from the Reading

1. Explain the difference between word pairs *advice* and *advise*, and *close* (verb) and *close* (adjective).

2. Define the following occupations: *author, carpenter, surveyor, publisher, orator, gardener, drummer, social reformer,* and *civil engineer*. Then ask students which occupations were Thoreau's means of earning a living at some point.

3. Discuss the meanings of *conventional* and *unconventional*. Ask students if people's ideas about what is conventional behavior have changed during the 20th century.

4. Point out that many words beginning with *co-* have meanings related to working together or bringing something together. Ask the class to compile a list of these words. They may also circle the ones they find in the reading.

5. Compare and contrast the word pairs *pond* and *lake*, *own* and *possess*, *borrow* and *lend*, *alone* and *lonely*.

6. Ask students to give the nouns made from the verbs *obey* and *disobey*.

7. Discuss the meanings of the phrases *passive resistance* and *civil disobedience*.

Activities to Accompany the Reading

Playing Word Games

Dictate the following words to the class: *attic, brief, destroy, freeze, lend, luxury, married man, obey, fact, complicated, survive*. Then allow students three minutes to write the opposite of each word or phrase.

Improvising Scenes

Have students imagine that Thoreau is telling some of his friends in Concord about his plans to live in a cabin by Walden Pond. Have one student improvise the dialogue of a friend who thinks the idea is crazy. Have another student take the part of someone who thinks it's wonderful. The student playing Thoreau must defend and explain his decision.

Using Maps

Find Concord, Massachusetts, on the map. Remind students that Massachusetts is in the section of the country called New England. Have students name the other New England states. Ask them why it doesn't say New England on the map. Point out other regions of the United States.

Discussion, Writing, or Research Topics

Ask students to consider the following questions:

- What is Thoreau's philosophy as described in this reading?
- Is there anything wrong with Thoreau's idea that less is more? Could you live the way he did? What would happen if you tried? Would you be happy? Would you be able to get the necessities of life?
- What can individuals do to protect or improve the environment?

Extension Activities

1. Read to the class Robert Frost's poem "The Road Not Taken," and compare its ideas to those at the end of this reading.

2. Read some quotations from *Walden*, and discuss them. The most famous ones can easily be located in Bartlett's *Familiar Quotations*.

3. Encourage students to experience solitude by spending an evening alone without using the telephone, radio, or TV. Then ask what they did to pass the time.

For ESL Students

1. Have students say the following pairs of words aloud:

   live / leave   very / berry
   wash / watch   build / field

2. Explain that the letters *-ow* have two common sounds. Then have students say these words aloud:

   own   cow   how   snow

3. Ask students how Thoreau's lifestyle at Walden Pond compares with that of the poorest people in their native countries today.

4. Have students describe the seasons in their native countries.

READING COMPREHENSION

A. Mark each of these statements *True* or *False*.

_____ **1.** Thoreau believed that in some ways, a poor person was richer than a wealthy person.

_____ **2.** Thoreau didn't want to work hard because he was lazy.

_____ **3.** Thoreau's life at Walden Pond was unconventional.

_____ **4.** Thoreau lived by Walden Pond for most of his adult life.

_____ **5.** *Walden* was first published during Thoreau's lifetime.

B. Answer these questions about the reading. Write in complete sentences.

1. Was Thoreau a hermit?

_____

2. At Walden, what did Thoreau use for fuel?

_____

3. What did he eat?

_____

4. Thoreau said that the moles in his cellar ate "every third potato." What did he mean?

_____

5. Thoreau said that he left Walden because he had "several more lives to lead." What did he mean?

_____

6. Which of Thoreau's ideas do you agree with most strongly?

_____

7. Which of his ideas do you disagree with? Tell why.

_____

READING COMPREHENSION (CONTINUED)

C. Mark the statements you think Thoreau would agree with *A*. Mark those he would disagree with *D*.

_____ **1.** You must work hard to have a successful life.

_____ **2.** Sometimes it's morally right to disobey a law.

_____ **3.** Human beings are superior to other animals.

_____ **4.** Nature needs to be protected from people who unthinkingly damage it.

_____ **5.** Expensive possessions can be a burden.

_____ **6.** Your life will be more enjoyable if you follow the social customs of your community.

_____ **7.** It's important to dress for success.

_____ **8.** It's important to have some leisure time.

_____ **9.** God's work is evident in the beauty and harmony of nature.

D. Find these phrases in the paragraphs indicated. Then write the nouns that the underlined word(s) refer to.

1. the two Concord authors (10): _____

2. which was never locked (12): _____

3. some were handmade (13): _____

4. It was like a picture (19): _____

5. That sometimes required (20): _____

6. Thoreau didn't bother them (20): _____

7. he considers to be in harmony (23): _____

8. They offer (26): _____

ATTRACTIONS *Teacher's Guide*
© 1994 Contemporary Books
A Reproducible Exercise Page

VOCABULARY PRACTICE

A. Use some of these words to complete the sentences that follow.

attic	journal	own
cellar	lonely	perhaps
companion	luxuries	possessions
conventional	masterpiece	scrub
hike	necessities	simple

1. *Walden* was Thoreau's _____, his greatest work.

2. When I pay off the loan for my car, then I'll _____ the car.

3. The things that belong to me are my _____.

4. Some of my possessions are _____, and others are _____, for example, my gold ring and my fur coat.

5. At Walden, Thoreau wanted to lead a _____ life.

6. I keep a lot of old junk up in my _____.

7. A hermit lives alone, far away from other people. But he probably doesn't feel _____ because he enjoys solitude.

8. _____ my brother will let me use his car, but I'm not sure.

9. Do you write down your ideas in a diary or _____?

10. Thoreau didn't live a _____ life.

B. Circle the word that best completes each sentence.

1. The opposite of *melt* is (freeze, destroy, survive, cook).

2. That's not a fact. It's (a luxury, an opinion, a necessity, a cellar).

3. Something that's complicated is not (simple, difficult, expensive, frozen).

4. A basement is similar to (an attic, a roof, a pillar, a cellar).

WORDS IN CONTEXT

What does each word or phrase mean in the paragraph indicated? Reread the paragraphs. Then circle the letter of the correct answer.

1. <u>boarders</u> (4): (a) pieces of wood (b) people renting rooms in someone's home

2. <u>manual</u> (5): (a) a book of instructions (b) a skill done with the hands

3. <u>interfere</u> (7): (a) cooperate with (b) try to stop someone's action

4. <u>admired</u> (23): (a) respected, looked up to (b) attacked and ridiculed

5. <u>retreat</u> (26): (a) to go backward to escape from an enemy attack (b) a peaceful, quiet place to visit for a rest or a change

6. <u>benefit concert</u> (27): (a) a musical performance to raise money for a good cause (b) a concert for the benefit of the musicians participating

7. <u>foresight</u> (29): (a) ability to predict the future (b) good eyesight

HOMONYMS, SYNONYMS, AND SIMILAR WORDS

Match each word in the column on the left with the correct word or phrase in the column on the right. Write the correct letters on the blank lines.

_____ 1. gather	**(a)** collect	
_____ 2. handyman	**(b)** maybe	
_____ 3. hike	**(c)** things a person owns or has	
_____ 4. perhaps	**(d)** long walk	
_____ 5. possessions	**(e)** tool	
_____ 6. scrub	**(f)** rub hard	
_____ 7. utensil	**(g)** person who can fix things	

PATTERN PRACTICE

The second sentence in paragraph 14 makes a general statement. The next sentence gives examples of that general statement, following the words *in fact*. In this way, *in fact* is used to connect two ideas.

Example: My uncle has a lot of money. <u>In fact</u>, he's a millionaire.

Complete these pairs of sentences.

1. Thoreau's cabin at Walden was very small. In fact, _____
_____.

2. At Walden Pond, Thoreau lived a simple life. In fact, _____
_____.

3. My friend _____.
In fact, _____.

PARTS OF SPEECH AND INFLECTED FORMS

A. Circle the word (adjective or noun) that best completes each sentence.

   1. *Walden* is a great (literary, literature) work.

   2. That little boy is a liar. He never tells the (true, truth).

   3. Be careful with that knife. It's (dangerous, danger).

   4. Most people are afraid of (dead, death).

   5. Thoreau's advice was to lead a (simple, simplicity) life.

   6. I need my car to get to work. It's a (necessary, necessity) for me.

B. Circle the word (verb or noun) that best completes each sentence.

   1. Your counselor will (advise, advice) you about what courses to take.

   2. Did you ever take your parents' (advise, advice)?

WORD PARTS

The word part *co-* means "with" or "together." The word parts *col-*, *com-*, *con-*, and *cor-* have the same meanings. Do you know the meanings of these words? If not, check their definitions in a dictionary.

collect	company	cooperate
combine	convention	co-workers
companion	conventional	

Now use some of the words above to complete these sentences.

1. I'm having _____ for dinner tonight, so I have to cook a very nice meal.

2. My friends _____ postage stamps and coins.

3. A _____ is a meeting of people who have a common interest.

4. Don't argue with your _____ at your job.

5. If we _____, we can finish this task soon.

PHRASAL VERBS AND OTHER IDIOMS

Reread the paragraphs these idioms are used in. The paragraph numbers are in parentheses. Then use some of the idioms to complete the sentences that follow.

figure out (11)	make friends (16)	raise funds (27)
be willing to (12)	take notes (17)	keep pace with (30)

1. I don't understand this math problem. I can't _____ it _____.

2. You should _____ when the teacher lectures.

3. It's difficult to _____ when you don't speak the same language as your classmates.

4. My dog runs so fast that I can't _____ him.

5. Would you _____ live alone?

ATTRACTIONS *Teacher's Guide*
© 1994 Contemporary Books
A Reproducible Exercise Page

ANSWER KEY

It's Colossal

GOLDEN DOOR

READING COMPREHENSION, page 3
A. 1. False. 2. True. 3. False. 4. True. 5. False.
B. 1. and 2. but 3. but 4. or 5. so
C. 1. It's 151 feet tall.
   2. Alexandre-Gustav Eiffel designed it.
   3. It's about a half-mile north of Liberty Island.
   4. Tourists go there.

VOCABULARY PRACTICE, page 4
A. 1. popular 2. tyranny 3. symbol 4. overthrow
   5. deported
B. 1. exhausted 2. irony 3. pedestal 4. restoration
   5. donated 6. favorite 7. harbor 8. colossal

HOMONYMS, SYNONYMS, AND SIMILAR WORDS, page 5
A. 1. isle 2. aisle 3. aisle 4. I'll
B. 1. f 2. a 3. d 4. c 5. e 6. b

PARTS OF SPEECH AND INFLECTED FORMS, page 5
A. Sample answers: a torn page, a damaged car, an embarrassed student, a frightened child
B. Sample answers: a torn book, an exhausted immigrant, a broken elevator, a forgotten or misspelled word.

WORD PARTS, page 6
1. pedals 2. suicide 3. deported 4. inspected
5. transportation 6. gigantic 7. pedestal 8. centennial
9. homicide 10. pedestrians 11. misspell, mistake
12. descend

PHRASAL VERBS AND OTHER IDIOMS, page 7
A. 1. a 2. b 3. a
B. 1. let go 2. put it together 3. clean it up 4. stands for
   5. fix it up 6. take apart

PATTERN PRACTICE, page 8
A. 1. embarrassing 2. exhausted 3. confused
   4. exhausting
B. Answers will vary.

PHONICS AND PRONUNCIATION, page 8
A. 6
   courage, generous, gigantic, baggage, damage, language
B. garage, pleasure, version, measure, television, usually

SKY HIGH

READING COMPREHENSION, pages 11-12
A. 1. False. He was climbing for the challenge.
   2. False. There's no definite height.
   3. True.
   4. False. They both survived the fire.

5. False. There were no skyscrapers in 1871.
   6. False. The mile-high building that Wright designed was never built.
B. 1. b 2. b 3. a 4. a 5. b 6. a 7. a 8. b 9. b 10. a
C. Answers will vary.
D. 1. O 2. F 3. F 4. O
E. Sample answers: 1. they don't like elevators or they are afraid of heights
   2. he has already proved that he could do it
   3. it's a famous building

VOCABULARY PRACTICE, page 13
A. 1. approaching, avoid 2. limit 3. trespassing
   4. automatic 5. survived
B. 1. fireproof 2. strange-looking 3. world-famous
   4. wind-resistant 5. skyscrapers 6. headquarters

HOMONYMS, SYNONYMS, AND SIMILAR WORDS, page 14
1. waste 2. waist 3. hire 4. height 5. quit 6. quiet 7. quite
8. story 9. story

PARTS OF SPEECH AND INFLECTED FORMS, page 14
1. climber 2. generator 3. sprinkler 4. skyscraper
5. visitor

WORD PARTS, page 15
1. self 2. not 3. one

PHRASAL VERBS AND OTHER IDIOMS, page 15
A. 1. b 2. c 3. d 4. a
B. Answers will vary.

PATTERN PRACTICE, page 16
1. the tallest 2. older than 3. the fastest, faster than
4. longer than 5. heavier than 6. the busiest

PHONICS AND PRONUNCIATION, page 16
A. light / right, lies / rise, flames / frames, climb / crime
B. 1. May 25th, 1981 2. 16th floor 3. 110th floor
   4. 103rd floor 5. fifth tallest

GATEWAY TO THE WEST

READING COMPREHENSION, page 19
A. 1. True. 2. False. It is the tallest arch. 3. True.
   4. True. 5. False. It covered 828,000 square miles.
B. 1. It's made of polished stainless steel. 2. It's at the top of the arch. 3. It's below ground, between the legs of the arch. 4. Most people were searching for gold or for cheap land. 5. It changed from wilderness to a developed area. 6. Development caused air pollution, the Indians and their cultures were displaced, and some of the natural landscape was destroyed. 7. Jefferson engineered the Louisiana Purchase, which doubled the size of the United States by moving its boundaries westward.

VOCABULARY PRACTICE, page 20
A. 1. plains 2. doubled 3. wilderness 4. tame 5. frontier
   6. gateway 7. arch 8. deceived 9. stretch 10. fragile
B. 1. e 2. d 3. a 4. b 5. c

HOMONYMS, SYNONYMS, AND SIMILAR WORDS, page 21
1. plane 2. heard, herd, plain 3. plain 4. miner 5. minor
6. new, knew

PARTS OF SPEECH AND INFLECTED FORMS, page 21
A. 1. depth 2. height 3. length 4. width
B. 1. high 2. length, width, depth 3. deep
   4. width, height 5. long 6. wide

WORD PARTS, page 22
1. extinct, westward 2. inhabited 3. toward 4. Explorers
5. Stainless

PHRASAL VERBS AND OTHER IDIOMS, page 22
1. get out 2. roundup 3. round-trip 4. trick the eye

PATTERN PRACTICE, page 23
A. 1. was held 2. was delayed 3. was designed
   4. was owned 5. was called 6. was invented
B. 1. It's 2. Its 3. It's 4. Its 5. its

PHONICS AND PRONUNCIATION, page 24
A. shave, shell, shape, shine, machine, sure
B. Answers will vary.
C. *Steel* has the long vowel sound.
D. long *a*: eight, long *e*: deceive, long *i*: height

HEADS OF STATE
READING COMPREHENSION, page 27
A. 1. False. 2. False. 3. False. 4. True. 5. False.
B. 1. He wanted to attract tourists to South Dakota.
   2. Dynamite was necessary because the rock is very
   hard and a lot of it had to be removed.
C. Answers will vary.
D. 1. neither 2. Mount Rushmore 3. both 4. both
   5. Crazy Horse 6. Crazy Horse

VOCABULARY PRACTICE, page 28
1. Granite 2. reservation 3. plains 4. figure, emerge
5. treaty 6. dynamite 7. incredible 8. forever 9. carve
10. models 11. repairs, crack 12. regional

HOMONYMS, SYNONYMS, AND SIMILAR WORDS, page 29
1. feat 2. feet 3. wore, war

PARTS OF SPEECH AND INFLECTED FORMS, page 29
1. sculpture 2. carving 3. damage 4. repairs
5. funds *or* funding 6. crack 7. drill 8. face 9. carver
10. leader, leadership

WORD PARTS, page 30
1. pneumatic 2. binoculars 3. incredible 4. forehead
5. untrustworthy 6. vision 7. foresight 8. repeat

PHRASAL VERBS AND OTHER IDIOMS, page 30
Answers will vary.

PATTERN PRACTICE, page 31
A. 1. on 2. above 3. on 4. below 5. between 6. in front of
   7. above 8. inside
B. 1. during 2. from, until, in 3. Since 4. During 5. on
   6. by *or* in

PHONICS AND PRONUNCIATION, page 32
A. 1. a mountain peak 2. a famous president
   3. four powerful fighters 4. federal funding
   5. a friendly person 6. a five-foot plaster model
   7. foreign policy 8. finished projects
B. 1. Please close the screen door before the bugs
   fly in.
   2. Stay close to your sister so you don't get lost.
   3. Hang your clothes in the hall closet.
   4. If you close the windows it may get very close
   (warm and uncomfortable) in here.
   5. The repairs on the car were very expensive.
C. his / history advice / advise please / police
   sure / surface truck / truce recent / result
   press / president crazy / crass zoo / sue

HISTORY IN STONE
READING COMPREHENSION, page 35
A. 1. False. 2. False. 3. False. 4. False. 5. True. 6. False.
   7. False.
B. 1. b 2. a 3. a 4. a 5. a 6. b 7. a

VOCABULARY PRACTICE, page 36
A. 1. permission 2. tended 3. isolated 4. reshapes
   5. superstition
B. 1. wildflowers 2. underwater 3. overnight
   4. backpack 5. businessman

HOMONYMS, SYNONYMS, AND SIMILAR WORDS, page 37
1. great 2. deer 3. sight 4. site 5. dear 6. grate

PARTS OF SPEECH AND INFLECTED FORMS, page 37
1. carved 2. hunted 3. trapped 4. visit 5. explored

WORD PARTS, page 38
1. extended 2. preserved 3. returned 4. discovered
5. embedded 6. unemployed

PHRASAL VERBS AND OTHER IDIOMS, page 38
1. e 2. c 3. d 4. b 5. f 6. a

PATTERN PRACTICE, page 39
A. 1. longer 2. older 3. largest 4. higher 5. better
B. Answers will vary.
C. Answers will vary.

PHONICS AND PRONUNCIATION, page 40
A. Answers will vary.
B. 1. More than four million tourists visited last year.
   2. No, Spanish explorers were interested in gold.
   3. Returned petrified wood is displayed.
   4. Yes, you can have your car checked there.

DISNEY'S WORLD
READING COMPREHENSION, page 43
A. 1. False. It's in Magic Kingdom. 2. True. 3. True.
   4. False. 5. True.
B. 1. c 2. b 3. c 4. d 5. a

VOCABULARY PRACTICE, page 44
A. 1. avoid 2. hum 3. risk *or* avoid 4. board *or* avoid
   5. fire 6. orbit 7. combine 8. share
B. 1. Orlando 2. tunnel 3. India 4. pavilion 5. prototype
C. 1. e 2. b 3. c 4. d 5. a

HOMONYMS, SYNONYMS, AND SIMILAR WORDS, page 45
1. message 2. launch 3. contains 4. satellite 5. accessible
6. bargain 7. haunted 8. simulated 9. refuge
10. nightlife

PARTS OF SPEECH AND INFLECTED FORMS, page 45
A. 1. access 2. adventure 3. amusement 4. danger
   5. happiness 6. imagination 7. nutrition 8. pleasure
   9. risk 10. symbol
B. There are five noun endings: -er, -ure, -ment, -ness,
   and -tion.

WORD PARTS, page 46
1. Animation 2. astronaut 3. prototype 4. audiometer
5. technology 6. monorail

PHRASAL VERBS AND OTHER IDIOMS, page 46
1. run-down 2. stands for 3. sound effects 4. headed for
5. year-round

PATTERN PRACTICE, page 47
A. Answers will vary.
B. Sample answers: 1. wasn't afraid to try something
   new 2. opened in 1971 3. is the primary launching
   site for NASA 4. is in the Magic Kingdom 5. films
   entertained millions

PHONICS AND PRONUNCIATION, page 48
A. audio, aquarium, medieval, mosaic
B. thought *aw*, cousin *uh*, court *aw*, fountain *ow*
C. Sample answers: fault, taut, gaunt, saunter, vault,
   nautical, laundry
D. beautiful, educational, huge, universal, computer,
   future, module, usual
E. 1. lunch, the 2. the Kingdom 3. haunted, animals, the
   jungle 4. The some, souvenirs 5. restaurant
   Point out that vowels in unstressed syllables are
   often pronounced like a short *u*.

Back to the Past

A LIVING MUSEUM

READING COMPREHENSION, page 51
A. 1. True. 2. False. 3. False. 4. True. 5. False. It is a
   copy of how it looked in 1627. 6. False.
B. 1. they separated themselves from the Church
      of England
   2. there was a great danger of fire spreading in high
      winds
   3. he was born on the ocean
   4. he wanted to preserve the history of Plymouth
   5. they didn't have forks and had to eat much of the
      food with their hands
   6. the Indians who once lived there had all died

VOCABULARY PRACTICE, page 52
A. 1. recruited 2. established 3. beverages 4. harvest
   5. introduced 6. profits
B. 1. a 2. c 3. d 4. e 5. b

HOMONYMS, SYNONYMS, AND SIMILAR WORDS, page 53
A. 1. peace 2. piece
B. 2. left, left 3. piece 4. tipped 5. left, tip

WORD PARTS, page 54
A. 1. re-create 2. transport 3. mistake 4. harmless
   5. malnutrition 6. interpreter
B. Sample answers: overseas, overeat, overdo
C. Sample answers: transportation, transmit,
   transcribe, translate
D. 1. governor 2. leader 3. sailor 4. colonist 5. tourist
   6. visitor

PHRASAL VERBS AND OTHER IDIOMS, page 55
A. 1. locked the Separatists up 2. turned them in
   3. made it 4. cut down some trees 5. grew up
B. 1. was supposed to 2. were worried about 3. agreed
   to 4. had to 5. were supposed to

PATTERN PRACTICE, page 56
A. 1. About 2. On 3. During 4. In 5. On 6. Since
B. Answers will vary.

PARTS OF SPEECH AND INFLECTED FORMS, page 56
1. attendance 2. burial 3. complaint 4. harvest 5. profit
6. proposal 7. settlement 8. survival 9. supply 10. wave

AMERICA'S HOME

READING COMPREHENSION, page 59
A. 1. False. 2. False. 3. True. 4. True. 5. False.
B. 1. a 2. a 3. b 4. a 5. b 6. a 7. a 8. a

VOCABULARY PRACTICE, page 60
A. 1. antique 2. oval 3. payroll 4. transparent 5. attacked
   6. imagine 7. installed 8. ceremony 9. protest
   10. mansion
B. public housing = residences paid for or subsidized
      by taxes
   crystal chandelier = a hanging light fixture adorned
      with cut glass
   recycled tires = something made from the material
      of used tires
   private contributions = money collected from
      nongovernmental sources
   bestseller = a book that sells a very large number of
      copies

HOMONYMS, SYNONYMS, AND SIMILAR WORDS, page 61
1. portrait, painting 2. hard, hardly 3. visitor, guest
4. Capitol, capital 5. Who's, whose

PARTS OF SPEECH AND INFLECTED FORMS, page 61
1. furniture 2. designer 3. aide 4. addition
5. requirement

WORD PARTS, page 62
A. 1. exterior 2. interior 3. excluded 4. rebuild, discard
5. international 6. undeveloped 7. informal
B. Sample answers: 1. self-important, self-help,
self-sustaining 2. drug-free, fat-free 3. all over the
city 4. two

PHRASAL VERBS AND OTHER IDIOMS, page 63
1. line up 2. look like 3. will fall apart 4. call in 5. took
place

PATTERN PRACTICE, page 63
1. will have my car painted 2. had them shortened
3. have it fixed 4. got my teeth cleaned

PHONICS AND PRONUNCIATION, page 64
A. building, business, daughter, design, folk, foreign,
guest, guided, honest, plumbing, through, well-
known
B. chiefs, knives, lives, roofs, shelves, wives
C. special, Ocean, chute, social, mansion, Michigan,
machinery
D. million union

JAZZ CITY

READING COMPREHENSION, page 67
A. 1. False. 2. False. They came from Canada. 3. False.
It is mostly Spanish. 4. True. 5. False. It is privately
funded. 6. True. 7. True.
B. 1. King Louis XIV 2. LaSalle 3. Canada 4. Andrew
Jackson 5. the Mississippi
C. 1. O 2. F 3. O 4. O

VOCABULARY PRACTICE, page 68
1. balcony 2. Crescent 3. entire 4. pirate 5. improvising
6. carnival 7. Voodoo 8. preserve 9. alter 10. unlikely
11. authentic 12. causeway

**HOMONYMS, SYNONYMS, AND SIMILAR WORDS,
page 69**
A. 1. c 2. e 3. g 4. h 5. d 6. b 7. a 8. f
B. 1. sea 2. bury 3. alter

**PARTS OF SPEECH AND INFLECTED FORMS,
page 69**
1. belief 2. burial 3. denial 4. entertainment 5. growth
6. improvisation 7. knowledge 8. value

WORD PARTS, page 70
1. It comes from Latin.
2. *carna* = meat, *vale* = remove
3. Today, carnival means a large public gathering with
entertainment, perhaps rides, and games.
4. It comes from Latin.
5. *im* = negative, not; *provise* = foresee
6. It means to do something without preparation, on the
spur of the moment, and without following definite
rules.

PHRASAL VERBS AND OTHER IDIOMS, page 70
1. turn into 2. get the ball rolling 3. warm welcome
4. sea level 5. in for a big surprise

PATTERN PRACTICE, page 71
A. Sample answers: 1. he defeated the British 2. the
battle was unnecessary 3. today, it is not a problem
4. it is not free 5. people of all ages enjoy it
B. It provided a good view of the river, and the river
supplied cooling breezes.
C. Sample answers: 1. it has many important historical
sites 2. it is only 100 miles from the Gulf of Mexico

PHONICS AND PRONUNCIATION, page 72
A. bird, birth, culture, curve, earn, first, heard, leader,
learn, settler surprise, transfer, word, would, worst
B. *ir, er, or, ear, ur*
C. bisque, descend, highland, huge, hour, Mardi Gras,
rhythm, pleasant, sausage, sign, spread, value
D. 1. no 2. yes 3. no 4. no

GOLDEN GATE

READING COMPREHENSION, page 75
A. 1. False. 2. True. 3. True. 4. True. 5. False. 6. False.
7. False. 8. True.
B. 1. a 2. a 3. a 4. b 5. a 6. a 7. b 8. b

VOCABULARY PRACTICE, page 76
A. 1. foghorns 2. Counterfeiting 3. denied 4. spawned
5. embarkation 6. published 7. exotic 8. expensive
B. 1. h 2. d 3. f 4. c 5. a 6. b 7. g 8. e

**HOMONYMS, SYNONYMS, AND SIMILAR WORDS,
page 77**
A. 1. passed, past 2. earn, urn 3. cells, sells
B. 1. g 2. c 3. d 4. a 5. b 6. j 7. f 8. h 9. e 10. i

**PARTS OF SPEECH AND INFLECTED FORMS,
page 78**
A. 1. Escaping 2. Boring 3. nesting 4. performing
5. arching 6. Spawning
B. 1. were built 2. was designed 3. was inhabited
4. were laid 5. were made 6. began to be used 7. was
discovered

WORD PARTS, page 79
1. confinement 2. Education 3. government
4. recreational 5. plentiful

PHRASAL VERBS AND OTHER IDIOMS, page 79
1. c 2. a 3. f 4. e 5. d 6. b

PATTERN PRACTICE, page 80
A. 1. Fish could be caught on the island, and deer were
also plentiful there.
2. Some Chinese immigrants were hopeful, but other
Chinese immigrants were fearful.
3. The veterans came home from the Pacific, and
they saw the Welcome Home sign.
4. People want a museum on Angel Island, but there
isn't enough money to build a museum.
B. 1. Prisoners could cooperate, or they could stay in
solitary confinement.
2. Reading books was a reward, and a family visit
was a reward.
3. The building could be fixed, or it could be torn
down.
4. Some people prefer to ride the ferry, and others
take private boats.

A WALL OF NAMES

READING COMPREHENSION, pages 83-84
A. 1. False. It was financed by private contributions.
   2. False. It is in Washington, D.C.
   3. False. There were about 58,000 fatalities. Another 300,000 were wounded.
   4. True.
   5. True.
B. 1. It is the most popular monument in Washington, D.C., and crowds visiting it in a single day sometimes reach 25,000.
   2. The war was unpopular, and the United States was not victorious.
   3. Vietnam veterans were never appreciated.
   4. The Wall reflects what is in front of it.
   5. It makes people reflect on the senselessness of war and the loss of loved ones.
C. 1. b 2. b 3. b 4. b 5. a 6. a 7. a 8. b
D. 1. Diane Carlson served in Vietnam (1968–69).
   2. The U.S. military pulled out of Vietnam (1973).
   3. Jan Scruggs raised $8 million to create a memorial (1981).
   4. Maya Lin won a design competition (1981).
   5. The statue of three infantrymen was added to the Vietnam Veterans Memorial (1984).
   6. At this time, there were 58,183 names on the Wall (1991).
   7. The Vietnam Veterans Memorial celebrated its 10th anniversary (1992).
   8. The sculpture of three women and a wounded soldier was placed near the Wall (1993).

VOCABULARY PRACTICE, page 85
A. 1. compromise 2. casualties 3. protest 4. donation
   5. wounded, disabled 6. sculptor 7. parade
   8. unanimous
B. casualties, disabled, sacrifice, wounded

HOMONYMS, SYNONYMS, AND SIMILAR WORDS, page 86
B. Answers will vary based on dictionary used.
C. Sample answers:
   1. disabled = lacking some capacity to perform a task.
   2. wounded = injured
D. 1. capital 2. Capitol 3. wounded 4. surrounded
   5. mourning

PARTS OF SPEECH AND INFLECTED FORMS, page 87
A. 1. sacrifices 2. designed 3. design 4. compromises
   5. surrendered
B. 1. memento 2. Memorial, remember 3. memorable
   4. memory, remember
C. 1. verb 2. verb 3. adjective 4. noun 5. noun

WORD PARTS, page 88
1. disabled 2. impossible 3. inscribed 4. endless
5. contradicted

PHRASAL VERBS AND OTHER IDIOMS, page 88
1. In the middle of the night, Scruggs got an idea.
2. The Vietnam War dragged on and on for 18 years.
3. Some people didn't come back from the Vietnam War because they were killed.
4. Scruggs ran the Vietnam Veterans Memorial Fund.
5. The Wall is made of highly polished black granite.

A RICH PORT

VOCABULARY PRACTICE, pages 91-92
A. 1. climate 2. Invaders 3. mansion 4. possession
   5. Sculptures 6. tunnels, narrow
B. 1. sandstone 2. sundown 3. headland 4. storeroom
   5. earthquake 6. horseback
C. Answers will vary based on dictionary used.
D. Answers will vary.

READING COMPREHENSION, page 93
A. 1. False. 2. False. 3. False. 4. False. 5. False. 6. True.
   7. True.
B. 1. b 2. a 3. b 4. b 5. a 6. b 7. b

HOMONYMS AND ANTONYMS, page 94
A. 1. gate 2. gait 3. weight 4. wait 5. right 6. rite
B. 1. agree 2. disagree 3. tourists 4. inhabitants 5. solid
   6. liquid 7. mansion 8. shack

PARTS OF SPEECH AND INFLECTED FORMS, page 95
A. beautiful, fertile, strategic, passionate
B. 1. strategic 2. passionate 3. beautiful 4. Fertile

WORD PARTS, page 95
1. relationship 2. defend 3. Dampness 4. surprised
5. cooperate

PHRASAL VERBS AND OTHER IDIOMS, page 96
1. b 2. a 3. e 4. c 5. d

PATTERN PRACTICE, page 96
1. was built 2. was solved 3. was played 4. were discovered 5. is played 6. were practiced

Sun and Games

NEON OASIS

READING COMPREHENSION, pages 99-100
A. 1. True. 2. False. 3. False. 4. False. 5. True.
B. Answers will vary.
C. 1. b 2. a 3. b 4. b 5. c
D. 1. 30 million (4) 2. 4.2″ in Las Vegas (8), 9″ in Nevada (Sidelights) 3. $1 billion (11) 4. $8 million (15) 5. 1946 (1) 6. 726′ (21) 7. 75,000 (26)
   8. 8.3 months (27)

VOCABULARY PRACTICE, page 101
A. 1. real estate 2. regular customer 3. residency requirement 4. over budget 5. parental consent
B. 1. casinos 2. neon 3. humidity 4. roulette 5. reservoir
   6. lure 7. desert 8. erupts

WORDS IN CONTEXT, page 102
1. b 2. a 3. b 4. b 5. b 6. a 7. b 8. a

HOMONYMS, SYNONYMS, AND SIMILAR WORDS, page 102
1. f 2. b 3. e 4. c 5. a 6. d

PATTERN PRACTICE, page 103
Sample answers: 1. you should go to the shore
2. you can gamble in Las Vegas 3. bring a lot of money
4. You can see lavish shows

PARTS OF SPEECH AND INFLECTED FORMS, page 103
A. concrete, glass, health, pirate, wedding
B. 1. gambling 2. wedding 3. concrete 4. glass
   5. parental 6. curious 7. pirate 8. erupting

WORD PARTS, page 104
1. reservoir 2. reservation 3. combine, connect, convention 4. extravagant 5. depression 6. revenue

PHRASAL VERBS AND OTHER IDIOMS, page 104
1. no longer 2. chorus line 3. in the long run 4. a piece of the action 5. big shot

ELVIS'S KINGDOM

READING COMPREHENSION, pages 107–108
A. 1. False. 2. True. 3. True. 4. False. 5. True.
B. Sample answers:
   1. He popularized a style of entertainment and music that appealed to young people. He was the first important rock soloist.
   2. His marriage failed, he gained weight, his energy decreased, and he took too many drugs.
   3. No, it isn't.
   4. They can see lavishly decorated rooms, a full-wall waterfall, a carpeted ceiling, and Elvis's awards.
   5. The dates of his birth and death, January 8th and August 16th, are very important.
   6. Answers will vary.
C. 1. More people visit Graceland than any spot other than the White House.
   2. Fans buy tremendous amounts of Presley souvenirs and memorabilia.
   3. A postage stamp was issued in his honor.
   4. Elvis combined African-American, country, gospel, and western music.
   5. Elvis's good qualities were devotion to his mother, God, and his country; his generosity; his humility; and his politeness.
D. 1. Yes, Elvis had a loving mother. She didn't want to buy him a gun, but, although she was poor, she bought him a guitar.
   2. Yes, Elvis loved his mother. He dedicated his first recording, "My Happiness," to her.
   3. Elvis tired of the publicity and lack of privacy. Some consider the quotation evidence that he faked his death and went into hiding.

VOCABULARY PRACTICE, page 109
1. anniversary 2. fans 3. grave 4. decorated 5. souvenirs
6. gospel 7. display 8. recipes, ingredients
9. impersonate 10. royalties 11. victim 12. entertain

WORDS IN CONTEXT, page 110
1. b 2. b 3. a 4. b 5. b

HOMONYMS, SYNONYMS, AND SIMILAR WORDS, page 110
1. f 2. e 3. d 4. b 5. c 6. a

PATTERN PRACTICE, page 111
1. Although Elvis was a very poor child, he was a very rich adult.
2. Although Elvis's movies were very popular with fans, Elvis didn't like them very much.
3. Elvis performed with an electric guitar, although he played the piano much better.

PARTS OF SPEECH AND INFLECTED FORMS, page 111
1. death 2. succeed 3. weight 4. weighed 5. burial
6. combined 7. success 8. die

WORD PARTS, page 112
1. careful 2. harmless 3. wonderful, awful 4. tearful
5. priceless

PHRASAL VERBS AND OTHER IDIOMS, page 112
1. hit 2. flop 3. took off 4. Settle down 5. downhill slide

ENCHANTED LAND

READING COMPREHENSION, pages 115–116
A. 1. False. These are not ethnic groups. 2. True.
   3. True. 4. False. 5. False.
B. Sample answers:
   1. American Indian culture is being preserved.
   2. it has beautiful scenery
   3. the air is clear, and there are large unpopulated areas
   4. the builder died before a usable stairway was built
   5. a tourist can learn about many different cultures
   6. this isn't a real volcano
   7. it has huge, beautiful, underground rooms and hundreds of thousands of bats
   8. he was burned in a forest fire
C. 1. mainly 2. They honor Christian saints with pagan rituals. 3. buffalo stew, steaks, and hamburgers, fry bread, piñon nuts, and cactus jelly 4. winding
   5. Tourists take the tram to see four of the earth's seven life zones in 20 minutes and look down on half of New Mexico. 6. except for blasts of flame
D. 1. b 2. d 3. e 4. f 5. c 6. a 7. h 8. g

VOCABULARY PRACTICE, page 117
A. 1. adobe 2. reservation 3. diversity 4. conducting
   5. rodeo 6. acre 7. Fiesta 8. solar
B. 1. Anasazi 2. pottery 3. saint 4. Geronimo 5. dances
   6. trapper
C. 1. cactus 2. scientist 3. nut 4. galleries

WORDS IN CONTEXT, page 118
1. a 2. b 3. b 4. b

HOMONYMS, SYNONYMS, AND SIMILAR WORDS, page 118
Pairs that mean about the same are diversity / variety, fiesta / celebration, warrior / fighter, winding / spiraling. Pairs that are different are raw / cooked, arts / crafts, breathtaking / outstanding, prehistoric / ancient. Answers will vary.

PATTERN PRACTICE, page 119
1. explorer, soldier, and Indian fighter 2. multi-story buildings, stations for observing the solar system, and a complex network of roads 3. Native Americans, Hispanics, and Americans 4. shops, adobe buildings, and narrow winding streets 5. bright, clear light; wide open spaces; and beautiful scenery 6. silver and turquoise jewelry, baskets, and blankets 7. food, architecture, and language (also in street names and churches)

PARTS OF SPEECH AND INFLECTED FORMS, page 119
1. bears *or* bear 2. bison 3. chilis or chilies 4. cacti *or* cactuses 5. corn 6. deer 7. galleries 8. lives 9. sheep 10. varieties

WORD PARTS, page 120
1. Petroglyph 2. explore 3. multi-story 4. outstanding 5. endlessly

PHRASAL VERBS AND OTHER IDIOMS, page 120
Sample answers: 1. I feel scared because something happened that threatened me. 2. People from many cultures blended into a common culture. 3. It's performed outdoors. 4. The scenery is beautiful, the weather is usually pleasant, and there are many cultural activities and sports to enjoy there.

ALOHA!

READING COMPREHENSION, pages 123-124
A. 1. True. 2. False. 3. False. 4. True. 5. False.
B. 1. Maui's brothers looked back at what they pulled up off the ocean floor 2. she was trying to escape from her cruel sister 3. they wanted the gods to assure them of good weather and good fishing 4. the military provided the islands with several airports 5. they considered it to be an obscene and politically dangerous dance 6. Hawaii is a blend of many cultures 7. the hull of the ship lies in 38 feet of water
C. 1. a 2. b 3. b 4. b 5. c
D. Circle 1, 2, 4, and 5.

VOCABULARY PRACTICE, page 125
A. 1. wrinkled 2. migrations 3. publicized 4. scholars 5. atolls 6. ukuleles 7. Geologic
B. 1. c 2. b 3. e 4. d 5. a 6. g 7. f

WORDS IN CONTEXT, page 126
1. b 2. b 3. a 4. a 5. a

HOMONYMS, SYNONYMS, AND SIMILAR WORDS, page 126
A. 1. e 2. d 3. b 4. c 5. a
B. 1. see, sea 2. weather, whether

PATTERN PRACTICE, page 127
1. Hawaii became separate islands because Maui's brothers looked back.
2. Hawaii is a mere baby because some of it is only 200 years old.
3. Natives worshipped Captain Cook because they thought he was a god.
4. Pele went from crater to crater because she was trying to escape her sister.
5. People were punished because they broke taboos.

PARTS OF SPEECH AND INFLECTED FORMS, page 127
1. surfed 2. will make 3. Did, dance 4. Have, skied 5. Has, woven

WORD PARTS, page 128
1. variety 2. inhabitants 3. geologic 4. television 5. elevation

PHRASAL VERBS AND OTHER IDIOMS, page 128
1. e 2. a 3. c 4. b 5. d 6. f

LA LA LAND

READING COMPREHENSION, pages 131-132
A. 1. False. 2. False. 3. True. 4. True. 5. False.
B. Sample answers:
   1. it has a mild climate and varied landscape
   2. they have great curiosity about movie stars and their lifestyles, and they hope they will get to see a star
   3. it is a great honor, will improve their future employment opportunities, and will increase attendance at their films
   4. there is a lot of crime, the air is smoggy, and there is too much traffic
C. 1 the Hollywood Bowl 2 Hollywood Boulevard 3 Hollywood 4 the city of Los Angeles 5 the county of Los Angeles 6 southern California 7 California 8 the Southwest
D. 1. being photographed in front of the Hollywood sign 2. earthquakes 3. beautiful scenery 4. wood
E. 1 The movie projector was invented (late 1800s). 2 Silent movies were shown in movie theaters (1908). 3 The first full-length film was produced (1913). 4 Hollywood became the center of the American movie industry (by 1919). 5 The Hollywoodland sign was built (1923). 6 The first talking movie was made (1927). 7 The first Academy Awards were given (1929).

VOCABULARY PRACTICE, page 133
1. outstanding 2. scenery 3. waves 4. climate 5. earthquake 6. pile 7. floods 8. tourist 9. curiosity 10. Coast 11. photographs 12. resident 13. highways, traffic

WORDS IN CONTEXT, page 134
1. a 2. c 3. a 4. b 5. a 6. b

HOMONYMS, SYNONYMS, AND SIMILAR WORDS, page 134
1. durable 2. smog 3. celebrities 4. tourist attraction 5. autographs

PATTERN PRACTICE, page 135
Sample answers:
1. the Chinese Theater, the Walk of Fame, and the Wax Museum
2. silent films, new releases, and wide-screen movies
3. popular restaurants, stars' homes, and Rodeo Drive

PARTS OF SPEECH AND INFLECTED FORMS, page 135
1. made *or* filmed 2. introduced 3. known 4. built *or* erected 5. scared *or* threatened 6. kept, given

WORD PARTS, page 136
1. <u>over</u>priced 2. <u>over</u>crowded 3. <u>over</u>joyed 4. <u>under</u>weight 5. <u>under</u>achiever 6. <u>over</u>slept

PHRASAL VERBS AND OTHER IDIOMS, page 136
1. no wonder 2. takes in stride 3. traffic jam 4. gets stuck 5. handout

WINTER WONDERLAND

READING COMPREHENSION, pages 139-140
A. 1. False. 2. True. 3. True. 4. False. 5. False.
B. 1. . . . it is often the coldest place in the United States 2. . . . it was often too cold to play winter sports outdoors 3. . . . the weather is very cold because it is indoors 4. . . . it can be easily converted to accommodate them 5. . . . the Minnesota Twins and Vikings moved to the Metrodome 6. . . . it created a lot of new jobs and attracted tourists 7. . . . are the nation's largest Twin Cities 8. . . . its dome is supported only by air
C. 1. c 2. b 3. c 4. b 5. c
D. 1. 150' 2. 55,500 3. 4 4. 350 5. 10,000

VOCABULARY PRACTICE, page 141
A. 1. retailers 2. severe 3. obstacles 4. cancel 5. extraordinary 6. Amateur
B. 1. f 2. c 3. e 4. a 5. d 6. b

WORDS IN CONTEXT, page 142
1. b 2. a 3. b 4. a 5. b

HOMONYMS, SYNONYMS, AND SIMILAR WORDS, page 142
A. 1. b 2. a 3. e 4. c 5. d
B. 1. whether, weather 2. site, sight

PATTERN PRACTICE, page 143
1. Mall of America is a place for shopping <u>and</u> entertainment.
2. The mall has stores, a miniature golf course, restaurants, <u>and</u> nightclubs.
3. Paul Bunyan could pull a tree out of the ground with his bare hands <u>and</u> break it in half.
4. The Metrodome is used for amateur <u>and</u> professional sports.

PARTS OF SPEECH AND INFLECTED FORMS, page 143
1. domed roof 2. concerned store owners 3. high-priced merchandise 4. an enclosed theme park 5. seated passengers

WORD PARTS, page 144
1. <u>inter</u>state 2. <u>mega</u>phone 3. <u>sub</u>marines 4. <u>metro</u>polis

PHRASAL VERBS AND OTHER IDIOMS, page 144
1. try, out 2. go along with 3. come up with 4. team up with 5. get tired of

Birthplaces of Ideas

EARTH MOTHER

READING COMPREHENSION, pages 147-148
A. 1. True. 2. False. 3. False. 4. True. 5. False.
B. 1. she was the youngest child 2. she went to college 3. she wanted to study the sea 4. it became a bestseller 5. he was orphaned 6. it controlled insect pests 7. she died
C. 1. a 2. b 3. c 4. c 5. a
D. 1. $10 2. $19.25 a week 3. 1951 4. 1948 5. 900 million pounds 6. 26 years 7. 1981

VOCABULARY PRACTICE, page 149
A. 1. aquatic 2. microscope 3. toxic 4. poetic 5. progress 6. forcefully
B. 1. robins' 2. children's 3. friend's 4. man's 5. birds'

WORDS IN CONTEXT, page 150
1. b 2. b 3. b 4. b 5. b 6. b

HOMONYMS, SYNONYMS, AND SIMILAR WORDS, page 150
A. 1. e 2. a 3. b 4. c 5. d
B. 1. borne, born 2. plane, plain

PATTERN PRACTICE, page 151
1. To describe World War I, Carson wrote a story.
2. To tell Carson about the songbirds, Huckins wrote her a letter.
3. To help her friend and her planet, Carson wrote about DDT.
4. To learn more about DDT, the government conducted hearings.

PARTS OF SPEECH AND INFLECTED FORMS, page 151
A. 1. finally 2. already 3. also 4. forcefully, quietly
B. final, forceful, quiet

WORD PARTS, page 152
1. <u>tele</u>phone 2. <u>bio</u>graphy 3. <u>micro</u>scopic 4. <u>dis</u>couraged 5. <u>de</u>scend

PHRASAL VERBS AND OTHER IDIOMS, page 152
1. extended to 2. involved in 3. take over 4. based on 5. spread around

DR. KING'S DREAM

READING COMPREHENSION, pages 155-156
A. 1. False. 2. False. 3. True. 4. True. 5. True.
B. Answers will vary.
C. 1. a 2. a 3. b 4. c 5. b
D. 1. 1929 2. 15 3. 382 days 4. 780,000 miles 5. 200,000 & millions more 6. 35 7. 29

VOCABULARY PRACTICE, page 157
A. 1. crypts 2. prophecy 3. racial 4. sculpture 5. transportation 6. assassinated
B. 1. despair 2. discipline 3. martyrs 4. arson 5. facade

WORDS IN CONTEXT, page 158
1. a 2. a 3. b 4. b 5. b 6. b 7. b 8. a

HOMONYMS, ANTONYMS, AND SIMILAR WORDS, page 158
1. c 2. a 3. f 4. b 5. d 6. e

PATTERN PRACTICE, page 159
1. He worked hard to change society, but he was against violent methods.
2. She had read Gandhi, but she hadn't read Thoreau.
3. They installed a new sculpture, but some people didn't like it.
4. The boycott was effective, but some people ignored it.
5. I would like to attend the Olympics, but tickets are hard to get.
6. He wanted racial justice, but he also wanted economic progress.

PARTS OF SPEECH AND INFLECTED FORMS, page 159
1. a fulfilled dream 2. segregated buses
3. high-powered hoses 4. saddened people
5. dedicated work

WORD PARTS, page 160
1. nonviolence 2. protested 3. inscription
4. desegregation 5. community

PHRASAL VERBS AND OTHER IDIOMS, page 160
1. Jim Crow 2. up north 3. mixed freely 4. checked into

THE HOUSE THAT WRIGHT BUILT

READING COMPREHENSION, pages 163-164
A. 1. False. 2. False. 3. True. 4. False. 5. True.
B. Answers will vary.
C. 1. 1867 2. Wisconsin 3. Spring Green 4. Louis Sullivan 5. two 6. three 7. 1932 8. Scottsdale, Arizona
D. Sample answers: wood and other natural materials, fireplaces, windows, privacy, cantilevers, concrete, indirect lighting
E. Sample answers: He didn't like box-shaped rooms. He didn't like buildings on top of a hill.
F. Sample answers: students are apprenticed, costs are low, students do professional and housekeeping work

VOCABULARY PRACTICE, page 165
A. 1. innovative 2. clients 3. despair 4. sophisticated
5. generation 6. fabrics 7. textures 8. environment
B. 1. client 2. scandal 3. quarry 4. patio

WORDS IN CONTEXT, page 166
1. b 2. a 3. b 4. b 5. a 6. b 7. b 8. a 9. b 10. b

HOMONYMS, SYNONYMS, AND SIMILAR WORDS, page 166
1. c 2. e 3. d 4. f 5. a 6. b

PATTERN PRACTICE, page 167
1. Wright added a birdwalk to the house
2. he designed buildings with a lot of windows
3. he established Taliesin West in southern Arizona

PARTS OF SPEECH AND INFLECTED FORMS, page 167
1. verb 2. adjective 3. noun 4. noun (gerund) 5. noun (gerund) 6. verb

WORD PARTS, page 168
1. A sympathetic person is nicer than an unsympathetic person.
2. You should express sympathy to someone when something unfortunate happens to them.
3. A unique idea is one no one else has thought of.

PHRASAL VERBS AND OTHER IDIOMS, page 168
1. d 2. c 3. a 4. f 5. b 6. e

WIZARD AT WORK

READING COMPREHENSION, pages 171-172
A. 1. True. 2. False. He grew up in Ohio. 3. True. 4. True. 5. False.
B. 1. He needed money to continue inventing.
2. Answers will vary. 3. He was a hard worker, he was persistent, and he was creative and intelligent. 4. The laboratories created new inventions, and the factories produced them. 5. The tourist bowed to Edison's coat to honor Edison. 6. It means that the works of a genius are primarily the result of hard work, rather than natural ability. 7. He used trial and error.
C. phonograph, electric light bulb, movie camera, improved stock ticker, legislative vote counter, improved storage battery, electrical generating station, kinetoscope
D. Sample answers: He burned down the family barn. He set a baggage car on fire. He spilled acid on his boss's desk.
E. 1. a 2. c 3. c 4. b 5. a 6. b

VOCABULARY PRACTICE, page 173
1. patent 2. bulb 3. nickname 4. battery
5. manufactured 6. Silent 7. genius 8. offered
9. concentrate 10. improved 11. phonograph
12. research

WORDS IN CONTEXT, page 174
1. b 2. a 3. b 4. b 5. a 6. a 7. a 8. a

HOMONYMS, SYNONYMS, AND SIMILAR WORDS, page 174
1. g 2. c 3. e 4. a 5. b 6. d 7. h 8. f

PATTERN PRACTICE, page 175
1. worse 2. better 3. worst 4. bad 5. worse 6. best 7. better

PARTS OF SPEECH AND INFLECTED FORMS, page 175
1. inventor 2. improvements 3. invent 4. concentration
5. created 6. annoyed

WORD PARTS, page 176
1. microscope 2. Phonics 3. phonograph
4. extraordinary 5. telegraph

PHRASAL VERBS AND OTHER IDIOMS, page 176
1. found out 2. trial and error 3. big break 4. caught on
5. dreams up

THE WRIGHT FLIGHT

READING COMPREHENSION, pages 179–180
A. 1. True. 2. False. 3. True. 4. True. 5. False. 6. False.
B. 1. It was near the ocean, it had steady winds, and it had a high sand dune.
   2. People flew using balloons or gliders.
   3. They flew their gliders as kites, controlling them from the ground, and tested the controls before actually attempting to fly them.
   4. Sample answers: They developed accurate controls, and they understood the effects of wind on a moving object. *or* They were talented mechanics and they had perseverance.
C. 1. They spent as little as possible.
   2. There is water almost all around the land.
   3. The plane didn't go up as high as they had expected.
   4. Birds flew much better than they did.
   5. The government refused to buy their invention.
   6. Some visitors are eager to experience flight.
D. 1. B 2. B 3. B 4. B 5. B 6. A 7. B 8. B 9. A 10. B

VOCABULARY PRACTICE, page 181
A. 1. engine, propeller, tail, wings 2. airplane, balloon, glider, kite 3. pilot 4. pioneers 5. reproduction 6. control 7. experiments 8. design
B. 1. affects 2. accept 3. loose 4. experts 5. mechanical

WORDS IN CONTEXT, page 182
1. b 2. a 3. a 4. b 5. b 6. a

HOMONYMS, SYNONYMS, AND SIMILAR WORDS, page 182
1. accept 2. right 3. write 4. hanger, hangar 5. effect 6. except 7. affect

PATTERN PRACTICE, page 183
Sample answers: 1. taking a cruise 2. good jobs for me 3. that I shop elsewhere

PARTS OF SPEECH AND INFLECTED FORMS, page 183
A. Sample answers: 1. built, sold 2. flew 3. left, went 4. slid, spun
B. 1. experimented 2. experiments 3. designed 4. controlled

WORD PARTS, page 184
1. reproduced 2. reproduction 3. biplane 4. discouraging 5. redesigned 6. unusual 7. aerodynamics

PHRASAL VERBS AND OTHER IDIOMS, page 184
1. e 2. c 3. d 4. b 5. a

A DIFFERENT DRUMMER

READING COMPREHENSION, pages 187–188
A. 1. True. 2. False. 3. True. 4. False. 5. True.
B. 1. Thoreau was not a hermit. 2. He used wood from the forest for fuel. 3. He ate fish that he caught in the pond, berries from the forest, and beans and vegetables that he grew. 4. He meant that moles ate about one-third of the potatoes. 5. Thoreau wanted to write and teach. Answers to 6 and 7 will vary.
C. 1. D 2. A 3. D 4. A 5. A 6. D 7. D 8. A 9. A
D. 1. Thoreau and Emerson 2. the door to his cabin 3. pieces of furniture in his cabin 4. the bottom of the pond 5. collecting firewood 6. the moles 7. the narrator of *Walden* 8. Walden Woods and Walden Pond

VOCABULARY PRACTICE, page 189
A. 1. masterpiece 2. own 3. possessions 4. necessities, luxuries 5. simple 6. attic 7. lonely 8. Perhaps 9. journal 10. conventional
B. 1. freeze 2. an opinion 3. simple 4. a cellar

WORDS IN CONTEXT, page 190
1. b 2. b 3. b 4. a 5. b 6. a 7. a

HOMONYMS, SYNONYMS, AND SIMILAR WORDS, page 190
1. a 2. g 3. d 4. b 5. c 6. f 7. e

PATTERN PRACTICE, page 191
Sample answers: 1. it was only 10' by 15' 2. he had almost no expenses 3. smokes a lot; he spends $40 a week on cigarettes

PARTS OF SPEECH AND INFLECTED FORMS, page 191
A. 1. literary 2. truth 3. dangerous 4. death 5. simple 6. necessity
B. 1. advise 2. advice

WORD PARTS, page 192
1. company *or* co-workers 2. collect 3. convention 4. co-workers 5. cooperate

PHRASAL VERBS AND OTHER IDIOMS, page 192
1. figure, out 2. take notes 3. make friends 4. keep pace with 5. be willing to